MIDGARD
BESTIARY

COMPATIBLE WITH THE 13TH AGE ROLE-PLAYING GAME

BY ASH LAW

KOBOLD
Press

CREDITS

Design and Development ASH LAW

Midgard Icons by Wade Rockett

Original Midgard Bestiary Monster Design Andre Araujo, Wolfgang Baur, Jobe Bittman, Logan Bonner, Jesse Butler, Matthew Cicci, Tim and Eileen Connors, Adam Daigle, Mike Franke, Michael Furlanetto, Scott Gable, Richard Green, Jim Groves, Marc Hergoth, Andrew Hind, Brandon Hodge, Tracy Hurley, Matt James, Josh Jarman, Clare Jones, Brian Liberge, Nicolas Logue, Jonathan McAnulty, Mike McArtor, Ben McFarland, Richard Pett, Karl Rodriguez, John Steven Schutt, Christina Stiles, Russ Taylor, Mike Welham, and Dan Voyce

Interior Artists Darren Calvert, Blanca Martinez de Rituerto, Jason Engle, Cory Trego-Erdner, Rick Hershey, Michael Jaecks, James Keegan, Pat Loboyko, Chris McFann, Jeff McFarland, Aaron Miller, Hugo Solis, Allison Theus

Layout Chris Huth

Editor Wade Rockett

Publisher Wolfgang Baur

Special thanks to Carrie Rasmussen-Law, Martin Law, and ASH's gaming group: Crystal, Daniel, Em, and Guy.

INTRODUCTION

IT WAS A DARK AND STORMY NIGHT WHEN I MET THE WIZARD IN THE TAVERN...

The wizard was Wolfgang Baur and the tavern was the AFK tavern in Washington State. And while I didn't fight any dragons on my drive up Interstate 5, it *was* dark and stormy as we gathered to celebrate the launch of the **Midgard Campaign Setting**. I had just submitted my first published-in-print article to what would turn out to be the last published-in-print issue of Kobold Quarterly magazine, and I decided to push my luck:

> *"Hey, this Midgard Bestiary. You could convert it to work with 13th Age's ARCHMAGE Engine."*
> *"Who would undertake such a quest?"*
> *"I could do it, Wolfgang."*
> *"Well ... okay then. Do it."*

And so it was decided. Equipped with the sword of spellcheck and the mighty hammer of infinite cups of tea, I started my epic quest. The results are before you.

I've picked 100 of my favorite Midgard creatures for you to play with; some I picked because they are iconic, some because they made me shudder in dread, and some because they are just plain weird, unique, or awesome. (I'm a sucker for living constructs.)

I've also added some monster-related story hooks, and other cool extra bits that round them out. Most entries have at least one magic item listed—usually something you can loot from a body, trade with an NPC for, or simply make from a monster's corpse. These are for GMs who are feeling generous. Not every NPC is going to have a magic item to loot, or a suitable bone to craft a wizard's pipe out of.

If you decide that a creature does have a magic item, let the NPC use it in a fight or at the very least give the NPC an extra d4, d6, or d8 damage on a hit.

Most fun of all for me was writing the lists of things that each creature might have on it—the contents of a gnome's pouch or just what sort of staff a Minotaur is carrying or what the goblin has in that flithy sack. Most of these items are not treasure (though you might get lucky), but are there to add flavor and spark your imagination. Just close your eyes and point at the page. *What is in the gearforged's diary? Where did the goblin get the star-charts and trumpet, and what is she going to do with them? Why does the owl harpy carry seventeen silk scarves?*

Finally, you'll find thirteen icons from the Midgard Campaign Setting by Wade Rockett. Player characters' relationships with these powerful NPCs will provide resources they can draw on during play—and draw them into a web of alliances, rivalries and schemes.

Slay! Loot! Explore! Run away! Negotiate! Trade! Try to survive! Meet interesting new beings... and roll initiative.

In short: have fun!

- ASH

100 MONSTERS

(With magic items, story hooks, and things in their pocketses.)

ALSEID

The alseid, or deer centaurs, are the graceful woodland cousins of the more boorish and pugnacious centaurs of the Rothenian Plains. They originated in the Margreve Forest, but today a dozen or so tribes of alseid inhabit the White Forest east of Triolo, and other groups live scattered across Midgard.

Nicknamed "grove nymphs" and "horned hunters", the alseid rarely appear outside the wooded glades they call home. They see themselves as defenders of the woodlands and view their forest as an individual and a friend.

Cutting off an alseid's antlers is one of the worst punishments one can inflict on a deer centaur and is reserved for heinous offences, such as treachery or cowardice when the forest is threatened. In the Ironcrags a tale is told of a band of dwarven explorers, searching the White Forest for the ruins of an elven city, who ran into a band of alseid renegades with their antlers sawn off at the base. Only two dwarves survived.

THINGS YOU MIGHT FIND ON AN ALSEID...

Bow, made from the finest woods. Longspear. Armor made from cunningly woven feathers. Rope of twisted vines stronger than any elven rope. Bracers of woven bark and leather. Woodland totem, whittled from the heartwood of a tree struck by lightning.

MAGIC ITEMS

Alseid Girdle (belt). A wide belt of green leather woven with leaves and grasses. You move easily through even the densest forest, and leave no tracks in forest or woodland.

Recharge 16+: When you kill a non-mook enemy with a melee attack, you heal hit points equal to 5x your level.

Quirk: Drink only rainwater, preferably directly from the sky.

ADVENTURE HOOKS

The Alseid Prophecy: An outcast alseid comes to the party for help: she is pregnant and on the run from factions that want to either deify or imprison her unborn child, depending on which prophecy they believe. Is the alseid prince she bears truly destined to found a great empire, or to lead all alseid to destruction?

The Gold Rush: Gold has been discovered near the forest homeland of the deer centaurs. Dwarf prospectors are flocking to the area, and wish to hire the party as protection from the angry natives.

Alseid Warrior

Renowned as great hunters and highly skilled with their bows, alseid can move rapidly through the forest and leave no sign of their passage. Though wary of outsiders and territorial, the alseid occasionally lead lost travelers safely to a road, provided they demonstrate proper respect for the forest. Disrespectful strangers, however, may chase the same deer centaur to their doom.

Level 3 troop [BEAST]
Initiative: +8

Spear +8 vs. AC—10 damage
　Natural 16+ hit: The Alseid may pop free and move as a quick action, gaining a +2 bonus to defenses against opportunity attacks as it moves. If the move brings the Alseid into engagement with an enemy it may make a *stag's charge* attack as part of the quick action.
[Special trigger] **Stag's charge +8 vs. AC**—7 damage

R: Bow +7 vs. AC—10 damage
　Natural 16+ hit: The Alseid may make a *hunter's shot* attack as a quick action.
[Special trigger] **R: Hunter's shot +8 vs. AC**—7 damage

Woodfriend: The alseid moves easily through even the densest forest, and leaves no tracks in forest or woodland. Tracking an alseid is a DC 30 check.

AC 19
PD 17　　**HP 45**
MD 13

Alseid Ovate

An ovate, an alseid shaman, sees to the tribe's spiritual well being and tends to the sacred oak at the center of their territory. Possessed of great primal power, the ovate ensures that the tribe upholds their traditions and treats the forest with respect. Ovates are always female.

Level 4 caster [BEAST]
Initiative: +8

Scimitar +9 vs. AC—14 damage

C: Grasping roots +8 vs. PD (1d3 nearby enemies in a group)—10 damage and target is stuck (save ends).

R: Woodland winds +8 vs. PD—10 damage and target pops free, and is blown to any nearby point of the ovate's choosing.

Woodfriend: The alseid moves easily through even the densest forest, and leaves no tracks in forest or woodland. Tracking an alseid is a DC 30 check.

Yew doorway: Provided the alseid is next to a tree (close enough to touch) it may teleport as a move action to any other nearby tree.

Breath of life: Once per battle the alseid ovate or one nearby ally may regain 10 hit points as a free action.

AC 20
PD 18　　**HP 54**
MD 14

Alseid Prince

Male alseid sport a pair of antlers that grow very slowly, branching every decade for the creature's first 100 years. The antlers indicate status and thus have great cultural significance. A tribe is led by a prince possessing antlers with 11, 12, or even 13 points. Some ancient stories say that should an alseid prince ever grow a 14th point, he could claim the title of Imperator and unite all the tribes of the forest. Alseid princes are invariably strong warriors, often highly proficient with spears, and command great loyalty from their subjects.

Level 4 leader [BEAST]
　Initiative: +8

Spear +9 vs. AC—14 damage
　Natural even hit: The Alseid inspires 1d3 nearby allies to make a basic melee attack as a free action.

C: Whirling spear +8 vs. AC (1d2 nearby enemies)—14 damage

In the line of fire: Once per battle, the first time the alseid prince is targeted by a ranged attack it can change the attack's target to a nearby ally.

Woodfriend: The alseid moves easily through even the densest forest, and leaves no tracks in forest or woodland. Tracking an alseid is a DC 30 check.

AC 21
PD 18　　**HP 54**
MD 14

ARBONESSE EXILES

Rarely seen outside the foreboding Arbonesse forest, the elves of the old Valeran Empire still train in the martial and magical traditions that once made them rulers of most of the known world. Arbonesse exiles travel the roads of Midgard either because they were exiled from the River Court for some reason, or because they're on a mission for their lords—typically to recover an artifact of their ancient empire.

SECRET TRAVELERS

Traveling Arbonesse know well the mistrust and hatred they often find among the empire's former servants and disguise their appearance with heavy cloaks and deep cowls. All of their people train to move swiftly and with little notice, at least compared to heavy-footed humans and dwarves. Those who serve as diplomats and emissaries often master illusion magic or disguises so that they may move freely, for their personal or their patron's gain, when not attending to their official duties.

FEY WEAPONMASTERS

The Arbonesse are unmistakable in battle, wielding fey blades and arcane magic to destroy their opponents. The spellblades and mages use elemental magic, harnessing frost and storm to barrage and hinder their opponents. Those who feel a stronger connection to the gods receive additional training and begin to blend the arcane arts with the power of the world around them, becoming versatile theurges. Even emissaries never forget their blade training, however, and carry a longsword with them as a "symbol of station". The schools and academies that teach these techniques admit only Arbonesse elves, who must swear to teach their practices only to those of elven blood.

OCCASIONAL ALLIES, NEVER MERCENARIES

The elves' legendary military might built an empire and still lies in the foundations of some of Midgard's oldest cities. When modern nations fight, they often seek the assistance of the Arbonesse, if only to ensure that the other side does not gain it first. Predicting the will of the fey is next to impossible, however. They rarely meddle in human affairs, and when they do, they seem to pick sides at random. Two things remain consistent: the Arbonesse are loathe to side with goblinoids, and they take great offence at offers of wealth. Few acts earn the elves' emnity faster than emptying your coffers at their feet.

THINGS YOU MIGHT FIND ON AN ARBONESE EXILE…

Sunstone and lodestone on opposite ends of a leather thong. Travelling boots with a secret compartment in the left heel and a small hidden knife in the right. Jangling pouch of low-denomination coins worn prominently on the belt, and a well-concealed padded pouch of higher denomination coins that don't jangle. Brooch or belt buckle with lock picks concealed inside it. Fake map, with a secret true map that is only visible under certain circumstances, such as when it is wet and being read by moonlight. Whistle enchanted to be audible only to hawks and ravens.

MORE THINGS YOU MIGHT FIND ON AN ARBONESE EXILE…

Tiny puzzle box that plays a beautiful, haunting tune when it is solved. Fragments of an old dwarven saga. Backpack whose frame and waxed canvas unfolds to become a small boat. Small tent made of bulette-intestine leather. Padded vest with coins sewn in. Disguise kit. Wand in a spring-loaded bracer. Folding saw. Elven trail rations. Container of spices (salt, pepper, vinegar, mustard, sargazo root, powdered yobrill, etc.) and a set of horn cutlery carved with pictures of stags. Ring that transforms into a lock-picking clockwork spider once per day on command (treat as *knock* cantrip). Poison capsule. Healing potion capsule.

MAGIC ITEMS

Valeran Steel Sword (sword, any type). This sword has been forged using techniques that haven't been seen in Midgard for centuries, and gives you a bonus to damage only: +2 (adventurer); +4 (champion); +6 (epic). Whenever you miss, choose a damage type (cold, fire, lightning, or thunder). When you next hit, your damage has that type.

Quirk: You believe that elves are superior to other races, ignoring evidence to the contrary.

Hexenblade (sword, any type). A steel blade with moving lines of colored energy curling and weaving across it. This weapon doubles as a magical implement—you may add the usual item bonus to hit and damage to arcane spells that you cast. Casting a ranged spell while engaged does not provoke attacks, provided at least one of the targets of your spell is an enemy that you are engaged with.

Quirk: You make sure that others keep their distance.

Cloak of Verdant Silence (cloak). To an observer the garment looks like an ordinary brown cloak. If you wear the cloak you see that its subtle green-brown hues shift like autumn leaves in sunlight. Whenever you make a skill check to avoid being seen, roll two d20s and take the better roll. If the d20s both come up the same, you become invisible for five minutes or until you make an attack roll. While you are invisible you gain +5 to all defenses (unless you're fighting something that doesn't care if you're invisible or not).

Quirk: Whenever possible, you prefer to sleep under trees.

Arbonesse Wand (implement). Valeran steel and Arbonesse wood in perfect harmony. The wand gives you a bonus to damage only: +2 (adventurer); +4 (champion). When you crit with a daily spell, you may cast an at-will spell as a quick action that turn.

Quirk: You carefully consider your words, weighing them for maximum impact. Sometimes these pauses are awkwardly long.

ADVENTURE HOOKS

The Sunrise General: A landslide in the Ironcrags has exposed the tomb of an Arbonesse general. Emissaries from the River Court have arrived to claim the body, but it is missing. The dwarves who looted the uncovered tomb are dying one by one, and though the deaths are all either sudden illnesses or accidents, the dwarves mutter darkly of a curse. The elves hire the party to find the body, for the dwarves will no longer deal directly with them.

The Valeran Crown Affair: An Arbonesse exile was caught trying to break into a treasure vault in Triolo—and a Valeran crown is now missing from the vault. The elf had an accomplice, but who? Where is the crown? The elf claims the crown was not in the vault when she got there, but can she be trusted? Who does the party suspect: the shifty looking kobold vault builder, the underpaid yet loyal minotaur guards, the heavily indebted owner of the crown, or the blind roachling servant?

A Debt Repaid: The elves of Arbonesse owed a favor to a player character's ancestor, and have finally gotten around to repaying it with the gift of a Valeran steel sword. In their hurry to return to the forest, they conveniently forget to mention that the sword was stolen from the captain of the Queen of Night and Magic's guard.

Arbonesse Exiled Mage

Her figure is shrouded in a cowl and cloak, but arcane power crackles around the exile's eyes.

Level 5 caster [HUMANOID]
Initiative: +12

Touch of thunder +13 vs. AC—18 thunder damage
Critical hit: The target is also dazed (save ends).

R: Lightning bolt +13 vs. PD—18 lightning damage
Natural even hit: The Arbonesse exiled mage can make a lightning bolt attack against a second nearby enemy, followed by a third and final different nearby enemy if the second attack is also a natural even hit.

R: Ball lightning +8 vs. PD (1d3 nearby or far away enemies)—12 lightning damage and 5 ongoing thunder damage.

Fey grace: The exile ignores any difficult natural terrain, moving with ease through dense brambles or across rocky ground as though it were well tended lawn.

AC 21
PD 15   **HP 50**
MD 18

Arbonesse Exiled Spellblade

The figure's features are hidden within a deep cowl, but his fey blade and aura of unnatural cold betray his fey heritage.

Level 6 caster [HUMANOID]
Initiative: +12

Frost blade +14 vs. AC—18 cold damage
Natural even roll: Make a second *frost blade* attack as a quick action.

R: Arbonesse bow +14 vs. AC—12 damage
Natural even roll: Make a second *Arbonesse bow* attack as a quick action.

Winter's gale: Once per battle as a free action the spellblade swaps position with one nearby ally who is the target of an attack. Recharges after use on a 16+.

Fey grace: The exile ignores any difficult natural terrain, moving with ease through dense brambles or across rocky ground as though it were a well-tended lawn.

AC 21
PD 15   **HP 50**
MD 18

Arbonesse Exiled Theurge

The theurge moves with a deadly grace, and you have the unsettling feeling that a pitiless goddess looks out at you through her eyes.

Level 7 caster [HUMANOID]
Initiative: +14

Long sword +15 vs. AC—24 damage
  Natural 16+ (hit or miss): Choose a damage type: acid, cold, fire, lightning, poison, or thunder. The attack does an extra 10 damage of that type.

R: Arbonesse bow +15 vs. AC—24 force damage
  Natural 16+ (hit or miss): Choose a damage type: acid, cold, fire, lightning, poison, or thunder. The attack does an extra 10 damage of that type.

Yarilla's blessing: Once per battle as a quick action the theurge can recover 25 hit points.

Fey grace: The exile ignores any difficult natural terrain, moving with ease through dense brambles or across rocky ground as though it were well-tended lawn.

AC 23
PD 20   **HP 70**
MD 20

Arbonesse Emissary

The Arbonesse are well known for their cunning. Their emissaries are notorious for it.

Level 7 archer [HUMANOID]
Initiative: +14

Long sword +15 vs. AC—28 damage
  Natural 16+ hit: The attack does 10 ongoing poison damage.

R: Arbonesse bow +15 vs. AC—28 force damage
  Natural 16+ hit: The attack does 10 ongoing poison damage.

Sudden reveal: The first successful attack by the emissary causes one target of the attack to become dazed (save ends).

Fey grace: The emissary ignores any difficult natural terrain, moving with ease through dense brambles or across rocky ground as though it were well tended lawn.

Fey stride: Once per battle as a move action, the emissary can teleport to any nearby location that it can see.

Arcane disguise: As a quick action the emissary can use magic to appear to be a different elf-sized humanoid creature. The emissary can use this to imitate other individuals that it has encountered (DC 20 check to notice that the emissary is using illusions, DC 30 to pierce the illusion).

AC 23
PD 20   **HP 70**
MD 20

BONE CRAB

Voracious scavengers, bone crabs live on crags and in coves near coastal communities, where they use their specialized chelae to crack open the bones and bodies of washed-up humanoids and feast on their flesh, marrow, and decaying brains. Centuries of such feeding have given them a collective intelligence.

Much like an enormous hermit crab, bone crabs inhabit the salvaged skulls of humanoids. They hide among discarded skeletons and washed up bones along the coast where their spiny, ivory-white legs blend in perfectly with the surrounding detritus. Due to the bone crab's specialized diet of decayed humanoid, it carries a dangerous disease, as many an unfortunate and hungry sailor has discovered. Victims typically suffer high fevers and delirium; few who manage to stomach a bone crab's unwholesome flesh live to regret it.

If denied carrion, bone crabs will hunt in packs, using their powerful legs to leap on vulnerable prey on lonely coasts. They drag such prey above the high tide line and leave them to fester in the hot sun before they feast. They can pick corpses clean in a few hours. Areas infested with bone crabs are littered with cracked bones and sun-bleached skeletal remains—the perfect hiding place for these predators.

THINGS YOU MIGHT FIND A BONE CRAB HIDING ON, UNDER, OR NEAR...

Fractured femur. Rusted anchor. Shattered scapula. Cracked clavicle. Wet rock. Tidal pool. Splintered skull. Dried seaweed. Mashed mandible. Rum bottle. Ruptured rib-cage. Old boot. Unattached ulna. Old hat. Scattered spine.

MAGIC ITEMS

Bone Crab Breastplate (armor). This bony carapace grows spikes in battle.

> *Always:* +1 AC (adventurer); +2 AC (champion); +3 AC (epic). *Recharge 6+:* When a nearby enemy hits you or one of your allies, add a cumulative +1 to your miss damage.
>
> *Quirk:* Brains. Eat brains.

ADVENTURE HOOKS

The Bleached Shore: The party is hired to patrol for smugglers. During their patrol they spot the smugglers holed up in a cave in a bluff above a beach littered with bones. Suddenly, swarms of bone crabs emerge and scuttle toward the party. The rising tide cuts off all retreat: the PCs must cross the bone crab's beach and join the smugglers in facing wave after wave of hungry crabs if they wish to last the night.

Bone Crab

A cracked skull arises from among the discarded bones and scurries forward on the bleached-white legs of the large crustacean that makes the cranium its home. It looked like a pile of debris and bone until it moved.

Level 1 mook [BEAST]
Initiative: +3

Claw +5 vs. AC—4 damage

> *Natural 16+ hit:* The crab makes a second *claw* attack on the same target.

Hive mind: If one crab is aware of danger, they all are. Sorry rogues: you can't Sneak Attack bone crabs.

Down among the bones: Spotting bone crabs lurking near, on, or under bones requires a DC 15 skill check.

Diseased: After the battle, each creature that took damage from a bone crab attack must make a successful easy save or contract white ghost shivers.

White Ghost Shivers

Those infected by this disease suffer high fevers, delirium and chest pains, as well as coughing up blood.

This disease starts at stage 2. At each full heal-up the target makes a DC 15 constitution check. A success moves the disease down one stage. A failure moves it up one stage.

> *Stage 0:* The target recovers from the disease.
> *Stage 1:* Target's maximum recoveries are reduced by 1.
> *Stage 2:* Target's maximum recoveries are reduced by 2.
> *Stage 3:* Target's maximum recoveries are reduced by 4 and the target starts each battle weakened (hard save ends). After successfully saving against weakened, the target is dazed (hard save ends).

AC 17
PD 15 HP 7 (mook)
MD 11

Mook: Kill one bone crab mook for every 7 damage you deal to the mob.

CARRION BEETLE

Used as pack animals and even mobile weapon platforms by the sinister darakhul, carrion beetles are massive burrowing insects known for their armor-like shells and potent digestive acid. Normally nonaggressive scavengers, carrion beetles become fierce adversaries when threatened. Under the goads of their imperial handlers, they make for truly terrifying opponents with a powerful set of mandibles and a spit of digestive acid.

SCAVENGERS ABOVE AND BELOW

Carrion beetles are a normal part of both underground and surface ecology, feeding on fungi, leaf litter, sewage, and the carcasses of large animals when breeding season hits. They often form symbiotic relationships with mycolids, darakhul, and related species. Many creatures in the deep underworld eat carrion beetles, and their exoskeletons, though too brittle for weaponry, provide useful material for shields and armor. Purple worms are their major predators and are said to swallow entire beetle caravans when they find them.

MOBILE SIEGE PLATFORMS

With a wide back, serrated spiky forelegs, and a narrow head, the carrion beetle is too large to ride on comfortably. It makes an excellent platform for ballistae and howdahs, however. Its thick exoskeleton varies in color from drab brown, tan, and black to shimmering blue-green, purple-green, and a highly prized yellow-orange.

  Carrion beetles have little society of their own. In the wild, they rarely gather in groups larger than a breeding pair with a small nest of offspring. Domesticated herds of 20 to 40 individuals are often used to clear fungal forests, scavenge battlefields, or devour cave lichen and scour sewage pits.

SERVANTS OF THE GHOUL IMPERIUM

Domesticated carrion beetles live more complex lives than wild ones. Most serve as simple pack animals. The darakhul train the strongest as war beetles, carrying ballistae and harpoons fitted with lines for use against cloakers and other flying foes, and often armored with protective strips of metal or chitinous plates fused to their exoskeletons.

  In late life, their acid is used to digs tunnels. After death, their exoskeletons serve as both animated scouting devices—ghouls hide within the shell to approach hostile territory—and as armored undead platforms for howdahs packed with archers or spellcasters.

THINGS YOU MIGHT FIND ON A CARRION BEETLE...

Saddle. Tiny fungal parasite. Empty saddle bag. Painted handprint indicating ownership. Bags of gold dust worth 3d20 gp. Maps of the area, annotated with marks indicating what may be secret tunnels. Fresh meat. Rotted meat. Rotted meat crawling with large grubs. Mining tools. Bottles of mushroom wine.

MAGIC ITEMS

Carrion Carapace Shield (shield). The shimmering blue-green shield distorts your reflection in odd ways. *Recharge 6+:* As a quick action spit a glob of acid into the face of an enemy you are engaged with, dealing 1d3 acid damage per level.
  Quirk: You prefer your food spoiled.

ADVENTURE HOOKS

Underdark Lights: The party has been hired to track down and return a stolen carrion beetle. The culprits? A blind kobold who has fallen in love with a destitute derro. The star-crossed lovers seek to flee their families on the carrion beetle and seek a place to live together.

Abomination: An undead carrion beetle has been fused with a ghoul to create a new type of monster. (Use the beetle stats, but double its damage and hit points. *Caustic jet* triggers on 11+, and does poison damage). Its necrophagus creator wants to see it in action against surface dwellers, and has chosen the party as test subjects.

Carrion Beetle

These huge beetles wear golden bridles and carry huge leather sacks of stone and guano. The endless line of them marches without stopping, and the air around them singes the nostrils with the taint of acid.

Level 5 troop [BEAST]
Initiative: +10

Mandible crush +10 vs. AC—20 damage
  Natural 16+ hit: Triggers a *caustic jet* attack as a quick action.

  R: Acid lob +10 vs. PD—18 damage + 5 ongoing acid damage
    Natural 16+ hit: Triggers a *caustic jet* attack as a quick action.
      [Special trigger] **C: Caustic jet +10 vs. PD (against 1d3 nearby enemies)**—10 acid damage and 5 ongoing acid damage

AC 21
PD 19   **HP 72**
MD 15

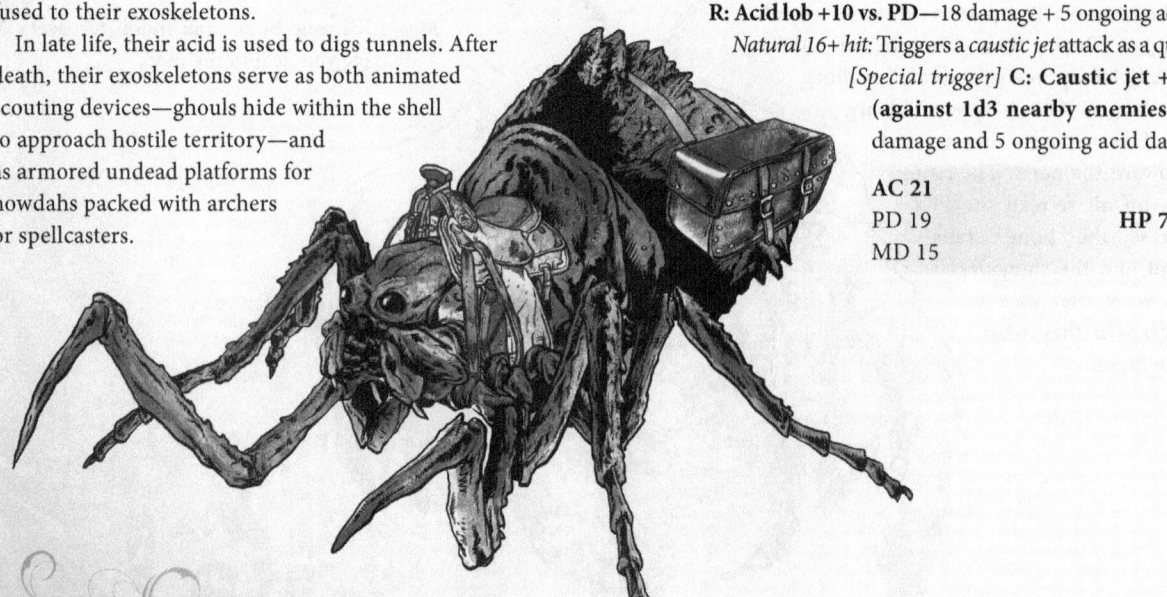

CLOCKWORK CREATURES

This construct looks like an animated suit of full plate armor with brass, tin, and iron pipes behind the joints. An unchanging face is set into its squat head, and it lumbers forward with a distinct lack of grace.

Large, metal constructs animated almost entirely by springs and gears, the clockwork form the heart of industry in Midgard's central cities. Though most commonly humanoid in appearance, many craftsmen will tailor a clockwork's appearance to suit specific tastes or labors. The quality of workmanship tells beyond simply shape, of course, and most of those clockworkers that are still operating after a few years are the work of masters. Many gearworkers design their constructs with multiple openings for ease of servicing.

Almost all clockworks have mechanisms and features that go unnoticed by anyone not familiar with the design. These may include weapons—such as the myrmidon's furnace or the hound's long tongue—but it's usually something mundane, like the storage compartment of most scullions. While often used to store the tools of its current task, these chambers are easily modified with special locks to conceal messages or smuggle goods.

HATED HOUNDS

Unlike gearforged, clockwork appear in many basic designs. While the scullion and its upgrades are very common, many other animal clockwork are also produced across Midgard. Of especial note are the clockwork hounds, remnants of Zobeck's darker past. First built to guard the aristocracy and hunt their enemies, Zobeck's secret police control nearly all the surviving hounds and use them to hunt down persons wanted for more aggressive questioning. In order to support, and sometimes better control, the hounds, Zobeck's authorities developed specialized clockwork watchmen to accompany them, called huntsmen. The outer plating of both types is most often painted matte black with mithral trim and occasionally outfitted with armor or barding for added intimidation.

Common folk detest them, and all but their keepers and commanders shun them. They remind everyone of Zobeck's aristocratic past, of the cruelty that kept it in power, and the similar methods used to preserve the current state. Some whisper that the huntsmen are not based on the watchmen but were developed in more desperate times by more sinister masters. If a remnant of their old programming remains, these people say, a sudden and violent clockwork rebellion may come some day. Any who might know the truth do not discuss the matter, for the hounds and huntsmen are simply too useful to the Praetors and the Council.

MAGIC ITEMS

Clockworker's Goggles (mask/head). A series of colored lenses that slide into position, revealing the secret flow of battle to you. *Recharge 16+:* Swap positions in the initiative order with another PC or NPC.
Quirk: You tend to stare at people for uncomfortable lengths of time.

ADVENTURE HOOKS

Cog Fighters: The Nine is forcing a clockwork mage to pay off his debts to them by creating clockwork fighters to battle in illicit gladiatorial matches. The mage hires the party to find him the parts, which involves defeating a lot of clockwork creatures and bringing him the innards. (If the party is more scrupulous they could play the opposite side of this adventure: they are asked to track down the madman who is sending goons out to destroy clockwork creatures.)

Firefly Summer: Fires are breaking out in Zobeck, and witnesses blame a strange new kind of flying clockwork beetle. In reality they are clockwork fireflies, the brainchild of an eccentric inventor who intended them to light the city's streets, homes and factories—if he can just get them to take orders properly. (Use the stats for clockwork beetle, but it flies and all damage is fire damage.)

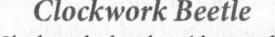

Clockwork Beetle

Clockwork beetles (designed in the form of various insects) often serve as familiars for gearmages and are very popular in Zobeck. They act as messengers, delivering letters and small parcels. Since they stay linked with their masters telepathically, they can even serve as stand-ins at meetings and lectures. Some of these mechanical wonders have been customized to deliver a toxin that can knock out a foe.

Level 1 troop [CONSTRUCT]
Initiative: +4

Bite +6 vs. AC—5 damage and the target starts making saves.
First failed save: Target is stuck (save ends).
Second failed save: Target takes 5 ongoing poison damage (save ends both the ongoing damage and the stuck condition).
Third failed save: Target becomes helpless (save ends the ongoing damage, and the stuck and helpless conditions).

Clockwork telepathy: The beetle can telepathically communicate with its master even if the master is far away. If the beetle can no longer communicate with its master it follows the last command it received for about an hour and then becomes dormant.

Perfect lenses: This clockwork creature can see in non-magical darkness as though it were daylight.

AC 17	
PD 15	**HP 27**
MD 11	

Clockwork Scullion

In Zobeck, hundreds of simple clockworks are in service at any given time, doing many of the repetitive, tedious tasks that keep the city going: sweeping the streets and courtyards, stirring alchemical pots and cauldrons for hours or days, turning fire spits in the kitchen, hauling water, mucking out stables, and so forth. These ubiquitous, and thus largely invisible, servants are sometimes used as spies or infiltrators.

Level 1 leader [CONSTRUCT]
Initiative: +4

Slam +6 vs. AC—5 damage

Patchwork Repair: Once per battle, one nearby construct ally can recover 5 hit points.

Perfect lenses: This clockwork creature can see in non-magical darkness as though it were daylight.

Nastier Specials
Unseen spy: The scullion has a telepathic connection with its master, even if the master is far away. While they are connected, the scullion's master can hear and see everything within the scullion's hearing and line of sight. It's important to note that "owner" and "master" may not be the same person…

AC 17
PD 15   **HP 27**
MD 11

Clockwork Watchmen

They are designed to keep the peace, and move with a tick-tock precision. Those who can afford more advanced servants often employ heavily armored humanoid constructs of bronze, iron, and steel as sentries and soldiers. Clockwork watchmen tirelessly patrol city streets or keep watchful eyes over designated positions. When engaging an enemy, they always offer the chance to surrender first, and will stop fighting if an enemy yields.

Level 1 troop [CONSTRUCT]
Initiative: +4

Halberd +6 vs. AC—5 damage

R: Tanglefoot cannon +6 vs. PD—Target is stuck (save ends).

Perfect lenses: This clockwork creature can see in non-magical darkness as though it were daylight.

Nastier Specials
Watchman's whistle: Once per battle if a clockwork watchman is staggered, it can summon 2d4 additional clockwork watchmen as a quick action with a piercing blast of its built-in steam whistle. PCs who know about this ability can disable the whistle with a DC 15 skill check.

AC 17
PD 15   **HP 27**
MD 11

Clockwork Hound

These beasts are wound a little too tight for their own good. Hounds sometimes operate alone, but usually they race into the streets as a party of three hounds and two huntsmen. Few can hide from these unsleeping and tireless trackers for long without magical assistance. The common folk hate and fear these clockwork beasts.

Level 1 troop [CONSTRUCT]
Initiative: +8

Mechanical maw +6 vs. AC—5 damage
Natural even hit: The hound makes a *tongue lash* attack as a quick action.
[Special trigger] **C: Tongue lash +8 vs. AC (1 nearby enemy)** —5 damage

Wound tight: When reduced to 0 hit points or below the hound makes a *tongue shrapnel* attack as an immediate free action.
[Special trigger] **C: Tongue shrapnel +8 vs. AC (1d3 nearby enemies)**—5 damage

Perfect lenses: This clockwork creature can see in non-magical darkness as though it were daylight.

AC 17
PD 15   **HP 27**
MD 11

Clockwork Huntsman

Black-plated handlers of the clockwork hounds, these huntsmen are distrusted by most of the living and hated almost as much as the hounds.

Level 2 spoiler [CONSTRUCT]
Initiative: +7

Pike +7 vs. AC—6 damage
Natural even hit: The huntsman may use the *net cannon* as a quick action this turn.

C: Net cannon +7 vs. PD (1 nearby or far away enemy)—Target is stuck (save ends)
First failed save: Target is stuck and hampered (save ends both).

Wound tight: When reduced to 0 hit points or below the huntsman makes a *cannon shrapnel* attack as an immediate free action.
[Special trigger] **C: Cannon shrapnel +7 vs. AC (1d3 nearby enemies)**—7 damage

Perfect lenses: This clockwork creature can see in non-magical darkness as though it were daylight.

AC 18
PD 16   **HP 36**
MD 11

Clockwork Weaver

The clockwork weavers resemble mechanical spiders with 10 (not 8) long, spindly legs. These small but useful constructs are a boon to the Honorable Order of Weavers as helpers, spies, and defenders. The spiders' legs include two that end in loops or crooks used to guide thread, six used for locomotion and positioning, one used for stitching and extremely fast needlework, and one large blade used to trim off excess thread or cloth (or flesh, as the case may be).

Level 3 mook [CONSTRUCT]
Initiative: +8

Bite +8 vs. AC—6 damage
   Natural 20+: Use *unmaking*.

R: Shuttle shot +8 vs. PD (1 nearby enemy)—6 poison damage and the clockwork weaver may move toward (and if possible engage with) the target as a quick action; the movement doesn't provoke attacks.
   Natural 20+: Use *unmaking*.

[Special trigger] Unmaking: One selected armor, implement or weapon that the target is using is considered 'unmade' until the end of the battle. The target takes a cumulative -1 penalty to attack rolls for each unmade item they are equipped with. At the end of the battle true magic items return to normal. Each item that is not a true magic item must save (11+) or become broken and useless.

Climber: This construct is shaped like a spider, and can climb like one.

AC 19
PD 17   **HP 11 (mook)**
MD 11

Mook: Kill one clockwork weaver mook for every 11 damage you deal to the mob.

Clockwork Myrmidon

Clockwork myrmidons are upgraded clockwork watchmen, heavily armored at their joints and most vital parts. They do not ordinarily engage in patrols or menial labor. They take the field in particularly dangerous situations and will defend themselves from attack, but will not initiate combat unless so directed. When they do enter battle, these unrelenting, single-minded warriors attack one target until that foe surrenders, flees, or is defeated. They usually attack the closest enemy unless instructed otherwise.

Level 2 troop [CONSTRUCT]
Initiative: +7

Heavy pick +7 vs. AC—7 damage

C: Flame gout +7 vs. PD (1d3 nearby enemies)—5 fire damage

C: Grease slick +7 vs. PD (1d3 nearby enemies)—Once per battle as a quick action, the myrmidon can cover 1d3 nearby enemies in flammable grease. Those foes gain vulnerability to fire until the end of the battle.

R: Flame jet +7 vs. PD (1 nearby or far away enemy)—5 fire damage
   Natural 16+: make a *flame gout* attack as a quick action

[Special trigger] When the construct is reduced to 0 or less hit points it *self destructs* as a free action

C: Self destruct +7 vs. PD (1d3 nearby enemies)—7 damage

AC 18
PD 16   **HP 36**
MD 11

DARAKHUL

A race of intelligent ghouls, the darakhul balance rationality with their eternal hunger for the flesh of sentient creatures. They visit the surface only when raiding. They call themselves "The People," and consider all other races either food or slaves. Though some darakhul seek a solitary existence, the largest majority have banded together to form one of the greatest subterranean nations in Midgard, the Ghoul Imperium.

A TWISTED CURSE

Darakhul arise when a particularly strong-willed creature is infected with ghoul fever and its anima refuses to shed its memories and reason along with its soul. Most survive the experience with their personality largely intact. Some necromancers claim that one can improve the chances of survival by deliberately infecting oneself and eating only living flesh. Only one person claims to have succeeded with this method, a necromancer named Uldar Ingreval, long since exiled from the Arcane Collegium of Zobeck.

GHOULISH APPEARANCE

The darakhul retains its memories and skills after death, gradually becoming ghoulish in appearance as fur or hair falls out over decades. Most commonly, darakhul only clothe themselves for practical reasons, such as the heavy plate of the iron ghouls. A few are vain enough to use wigs or magic to maintain the pretense of a living appearance, a practice quite common among the necrophagi.

RULE OF THE NECROPHAGI

The ghouls of the Imperium do not rule solely through their strength in battle or terrible hunger. They also employ the dark arts of necromancy and demonology to increase their power in the subterranean realms beneath the Principality of Morgau and Doresh. The Imperium's twisted arcanists are known collectively as the lore cult of the necrophagi, which though it seems superficially similar to a faith, is based on the use of arcane and necromantic knowledge rather than religion.

The darakhul have had an uneasy relationship with necromancers and the practice of necromancy from the beginning. After all, they are competing for the same limited supply of corpses. Many darakhul have studied and mastered this magic, and they consider necromancers rivals worth absorbing into the empire. As a result, the darakhul arcanist tradition is quite strong.

The ghoulish necrophagi of the Imperium practice necromancy using the materials they have available, primarily the bones and bodies of non-humanoid creatures. Some work on small, useful undead servants—mostly skeletons and zombies—while others work on powerful war machines. They are the technologists of the Imperium, and are respected for that reason. Their mark is a triple skull.

PERFECTED CORRUPTION

Through long starvation, a ghoul may achieve a powdery form and become a bonepowder ghoul. The process invariably takes decades, which is why so few bonepowder ghouls exist. The few ghouls who can show such self-restraint are highly respected among their peers, for all ghouls know the drive of hunger. Indeed, using hunger as a form of torture is considered offensive to the ways of the Imperium. This isn't to say that it never happens, and thus bonepowder ghouls may rise from unintended circumstances. A starved prisoner or a ghoul trapped in a sealed-off cavern might leave behind most of its remnant flesh and become animated almost purely by hunger, hatred, and the wisdom of long centuries in which to plot the destruction of its enemies.

THINGS YOU MIGHT FIND ON A DARAKHUL…

Iron key on a chain. Spiked throwing-lantern. Leather map that looks like it shows a back way into an underground prison. Canvas hand-wrappings, their outer surface studded with spikes and broken glass, and their fabric soaked with blood. Thin strips of gold and silver, melted down from jewelry taken from victims (2d10x10 gp). Several sets of iron manacles. 49½ feet of rope. Butcher's hook. Half eaten dwarven foot, in a pickle jar. Backpack made of woven elf-skin leather strips. Whip made from braided hair and knuckle bones. Sharp iron claw-sheaths. Banded-metal armor (held in place with hooks). Thongs and belts from which hang cleavers and flensing knives. Pouch of salt.

MAGIC ITEMS

Ghoul-Face Shield (shield). The snarling face of this leather-covered shield is still alive—or at least as alive as a ghoul ever is—and it bites back. *Recharge 16+:* When you are hit in melee combat you deal your basic melee miss damage to the enemy that hit you. *Quirk:* The shield wants fresh meat. Feed fresh meat to your shield.

ADVENTURE HOOKS

Ghoul's Bounty: The party is hired to penetrate deep into ghoul-controlled territory to kill six specific ghouls, for a huge bounty. They don't know that this is a political assassination and their true employer is a necrophagus savant who only cares about one of the six targets—the rest are distractions to conceal his intent.

Modern Times: A Zobeck clockworks manufacturer is outperforming all its rivals, and a competitor hires the party to find out how they can produce so many items at such an astounding rate. Their secret? Enslaved ghoul labor. Word of this has reached the Ghoul Emperor, and he's sent a party of ghouls led by an imperial ghast centurion to free the slaves, and burn down the entire quarter as retribution.

Darakhul Citizen

"So, which are you? Food? Or slave?"

Level 3 mook [UNDEAD]
Initiative: +6
Vulnerable: holy

Tearing claws +6 vs. AC—6 damage

Vicious bite +6 vs. AC—4 damage and the target is stuck (save ends). If the target is already stuck, it becomes stunned (save ends both effects).

Ghoulish resistance: Resist negative energy and poison 16+. When a negative energy or poison attack targets this creature, the attacker must roll a natural 16+ on the attack roll or it only deals half damage.

AC 19
PD 17   **HP 11 (mook)**
MD 13

Mook: Kill one darakhul citizen mook for every 11 damage you deal to the mob.

Iron Ghoul

The darakhul are normally naked, but these sport iron bands and sharpened gauntlets. Ghouls always look hungry, but these…look **really** *hungry.*

Double strength level 4 wrecker [UNDEAD]
Initiative: +8
Vulnerable: holy

Tearing claws +6 vs. AC—28 damage
Blind savagery: When the ghoul is hit by an opportunity attack it makes an immediate *tearing claws* attack against the triggering creature as a free action. This attack crits on an 18+.

Vicious bite +6 vs. AC—20 damage and the target is stuck (save ends). If the target is already stuck, it becomes stunned (save ends both effects).

Brutal steel +6 vs. AC—15 damage and the target is vulnerable until the end of its next turn.

Savage assault: When the escalation die is odd the ghoul can perform an extra attack or a move action (including burrowing) as a quick action. It can make a maximum of two attacks per turn when using this ability.

Crushing mountain: On a natural even melee attack roll the iron ghoul may pop the target free of engagement. The iron ghoul can never be popped free of engagement.

Grave burrower: An iron ghoul can use its claws to burrow, moving at its normal movement rate under the ground.

Ghoulish resistance: Resist negative energy and poison 16+. When a negative energy or poison attack targets this creature, the attacker must roll a natural 16+ on the attack roll or it only deals half damage.

AC 20
PD 18   **HP 108**
MD 14

Necrophagus Savant

The desiccated creature looks up from picking over the remains of a human ribcage with the air of a disturbed nobleman. It seems almost amused at the intrusion, and at a wave of its stained hand, six more such creatures step from the darkness with crossbows leveled and full plate gleaming.

Double strength level 6 leader [UNDEAD]
Initiative: +15
Vulnerable: holy

Shadow claws +11 vs. AC—30 damage and 7 ongoing negative energy damage (save ends).

Vicious bite +11 vs. AC—18 damage and the target is stuck (save ends). If the target is already stuck, it becomes stunned (save ends both effects).

continued overleaf…

R: Grave's pallor +11 vs. PD—10 ongoing negative energy damage. Each failed save by the target against the ongoing damage increases the amount of ongoing damage by 10.
Limited use: Once per battle.

R: Pull the strings +11 vs. MD (all nearby or far away enemies that are currently hampered or helpless)—Each target hit loses any conditions on it, and becomes confused (save ends).
Limited use: Once per battle.

Blood casting: Using *shadow claws* or *vicious bite*, the ghoul removes vital organs from a dead or dying creature in order to enhance its magic (treat as a coup de grace if the creature is still making death saves). Consuming the organs as a quick action before the end of the encounter grants a +1 bonus to the ghoul's next attack roll and if the attack hits, treats the damage as if it was a critical hit. The organs can be kept for up to 24 hours, but any organs consumed after the encounter in which they were harvested grants only a +1 bonus to the next attack roll.

Spelleater: Using *shadow claws* or *vicious bite*, the ghoul removes vital organs from a dead or dying spellcaster in order to enhance its magic (treat as a coup de grace if the spellcaster is still making death saves). Consuming the organs as a quick action before the end of the encounter grants the ghoul the ability to use one of the creature's spells that the creature was still able to use at the time of death. The ghoul may now use that spell once. Treat the spell as cast by the original creature. The spell is lost after use, but any number of these spells can be collected.

Reanimate the fallen (Recharge 16+): Once per battle 1d3 nearby creatures with 0 hit points or less, and whose total levels do not exceed 6, regain half their total hit points as temporary hit points. The reanimated creatures act under the control of the necrophagus savant. If the necrophagus releases control of them, or if the necrophagus is destroyed, the creature loses its temporary hit points.

Ghoulish resistance: Resist negative energy and poison 16+. When a negative energy or poison attack targets this creature, the attacker must roll a natural 16+ on the attack roll or it only deals half damage.

AC 22
PD 19   **HP 180**
MD 19

Bonepowder Ghoul

The bonepowder ghoul is small and unassuming, a pile of dust and bone fragments that resembles a destroyed mummy or the remnants of a vampire burned by sunlight. Then the dust stirs and rises into the air, even though there is no wind. Within the whirlwind that forms, a death-mask of a face looks out at you and opens its jaws wide.

Double strength level 8 spoiler [UNDEAD]
Initiative: +17
Vulnerable: holy

Jaws of dust +13 vs. AC—60 damage and target is stuck (save ends). If the target is already stuck it also becomes stunned (save ends).
   Natural 16+ hit or miss: *Grave dance* is triggered.

C: Font of death +13 vs. PD (1d3 nearby enemies)—25 damage, the target is weakened until the end of its next turn, and the ghoul gains 30 hit points
   Natural 16+ hit or miss: *Grave dance* is triggered.

[Special trigger] *Grave dance:* The ghoul makes an attack +13 vs. MD against all nearby enemies, targeting the enemy among them with the highest Mental Defense. If it succeeds it teleports to any place nearby or far away that it can see, and becomes hidden until it moves or attacks (DC 30 to spot it).

Ghoul form: The bonepowder ghoul can take the form of a swirling whirlwind or a small humanoid. Even when a bonepowder ghoul is in humanoid form, hearing its voice requires a DC 20 check if you are not yourself undead and it does not intend for you to hear it.

Hidden vantage: The bonepowder ghoul deals +20 damage to any enemy that is engaged with an ally.

Dulled senses: Nearby living creatures take a -4 penalty to skill checks and initiative rolls.

Bone whirlwind: A foe who staggers the bonepowder ghoul or reduces its hit points to 0 or less takes 20 ongoing negative energy damage and becomes weakened (save ends both).

Ghoulish resistance: Resist negative energy and poison 16+. When a negative energy or poison attack targets this creature, the attacker must roll a natural 16+ on the attack roll or it only deals half damage.

AC 24
PD 21   **HP 288**
MD 21

DEADLY MOSSES

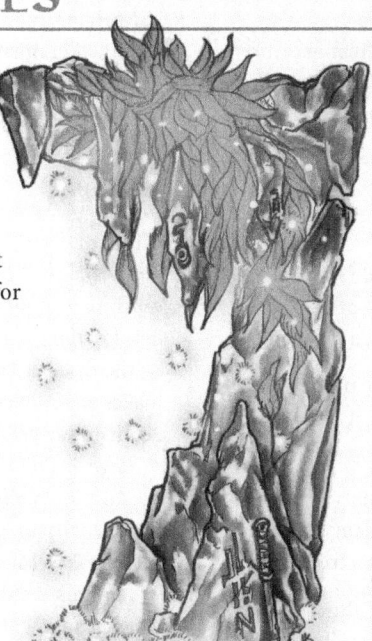

A patch of tangled, lacy moss clings to the ceiling above, slowly pulsing with an eerie glow. Among the soft, feathery mass, stems gently writhe, periodically dusting the ground below with a twinkling of phosphorescent spores.

Appearing as a large patch of bioluminescent flora, cavelight moss is frequently mistaken for a benign plant. In fact, this creature savors the taste of living flesh and renders its meal immobile before starting the long process of digestion. Cavelight moss glows with a pale, yet warm, yellow light. When agitated, the light emitted changes to a cold blue.

SLOW-MOVING KILLERS

Like normal moss, cavelight moss is a collection of smaller life forms patched together and sharing sensations. Barely cognitive, cavelight moss spends its time positioning itself above well-traveled sections of caverns and mostly feeds on cave rats, snared bats, and crawling insects. When cavelight moss becomes aware of larger prey, it begins the slow and arduous task of quietly moving toward the larger creatures, staying safely outside any main area of habitation.

GLOWING GUARDIANS

While most underground denizens understand the dangers of cavelight moss and seek to eradicate it when found, some cunning cave dwellers cultivate the moss in their hunting grounds and ambush those it ensnares. Some races even transplant the moss to their home caverns and use the plants as crude watchdogs. Cavelight moss attempts to remain as unobtrusive as possible until prey approaches within reach.

LIFE COMES FROM DEATH

Cavelight moss lives a simple existence, and when in a safe area inhabited by weak animals, it can survive for close to 200 years. The spores from a cavelight moss glow like their parent, and if a particular specimen stays in place for several decades, the place may glow for years after its death. If flesh and blood creatures die in such an area, the spores can germinate and grow in the carrion. In lean times, these spores can grow, albeit slowly, on guano or other materials rich in moisture and organic nutrients.

MINDROT MUTATIONS

Anyone who learns the dangers of cavelight moss versus a harmless, phosphorescent growth might be surprised when they encounter the mindrot moss. This creature, when docile, looks almost exactly like the lesser cavelight moss, requiring a DC 35 skill check to identify properly. When agitated, the difference becomes more apparent, as the moss loses spores and glows with an eerie violet hue.

Like its less-dangerous relative, mindrot moss is a parasite that consumes the bodies of mortal creatures in order to replicate. When inhaled, mindrot spores enter the bloodstream and attempt to take root in the brain.

MINDROT THRALLS

As the fungus grows it secretes an acid that dissolves the body of the host, slowly replacing the creature's flesh with its own as it feeds and multiplies. The fungus first destroys the parts of the brain that control motor functions, taking over the creature's movement so that the victim loses control of its actions even while alive and aware of what is happening.

Eventually the fungus burns away all of the victim's flesh, covering the skeleton of the creature with its own fibrous tissue in a ghastly caricature of its host. Intelligent creatures (humanoid thralls) often cover themselves in thick robes or layers of cloth to travel undetected. Uncovered, the thrall resembles a gaunt version of the unfortunate host, except its taut, waxy skin bubbles with bursting spore pods. If the creature cannot infect a new victim within a few weeks of completely consuming its current host, it starves and eventually dies. The starved corpse of a mindrot thrall slowly dissolves into a crusted skeleton.

PRODUCT OF THE WASTES

Some wizards whisper that the fungus came to Midgard on the back of one of the shambling, otherworldly horrors that haunt the Wasted West. Its origin in that inhospitable desert is likely the only reason this insidious creature has not destroyed whole cities through infection, though the fungus is ever searching for hosts that will carry it to where it can spread freely.

MAGIC ITEMS

Mindrot Potion (potion). Created from dangerous mosses, this glowing brew aids where healing potions cannot. When drunk it grants an automatic success to the next death save made that day; but after that save is made, the drinker takes a -1 penalty to MD until their next full rest.

ADVENTURE HOOKS

Night of the Thralls: An opera house has collapsed into a sinkhole. The following night the first of the mindrot thralls, still dressed opera-going finery, crawls up out of the sewers. As a riot breaks out, do the adventurers find a safe place to hole up until dawn, use this opportunity to loot, or protect the innocents caught in the madness?

A Rare Vintage: A wealthy merchant or aristocrat with exotic tastes is due to hold a dinner party, and hires the adventurers to fetch a ton of cavelight moss for the staff to convert into glowing wine. But a vengeful alchemist from Maillon intends to taint the shipment with a potion that will give the wine the property of mindrot fungus. Will the PCs discover and foil the plan? Or will the dinner party take a ghastly turn?

Cavelight Moss

The tangled glowing moss is far from benign. Some adventurers carry lanterns full of the stuff; but feeding your lantern blood to keep it lit is never a good long-term plan, especially if the moss escapes.

Level 3 troop [PLANT]
Initiative: +3
Vulnerability: Fire

Tendrils +8 vs. AC—6 damage and target is dazed (save ends).
 Natural 16+ hit: Target takes 12 damage instead of 6.
 Natural 18+ hit: Target is stunned instead of dazed (save ends).

Phosphorescent: The moss glows dimly. The first time it takes damage in a battle it lights up so brightly that it stuns (save ends) the nearest enemy that can see it.

Crawling horror: The moss can only move on rounds where the escalation die is odd. Whenever it takes holy damage it may immediately pop free of engagement and move as a free action.

Resist psychic 16+: When a psychic attack targets this creature, the attacker must roll a natural 16+ on the attack roll or it only deals half damage.

AC 19
PD 17   **HP 45**
MD 13

Mindrot Moss

One wouldn't think that simple moss could pack so much of a punch... but it is the infection for which the moss is named that is the real danger. It is very easy to mistake mindrot moss for cavelight moss.

Level 7 wrecker [PLANT]
Initiative: +7
Vulnerability: Fire

Mossy tendril +12 vs. AC—20 damage
 Natural 14+ hit or miss: Make a second *mossy tendril* attack as a quick action.
 Natural 16+ hit: 5 ongoing acid damage and target is stuck (save ends both).
 [special] If two mossy tendril attacks hit the same target in the same round the target is helpless (save ends) and must make an additional save at the start of each turn that they are helpless or become infected with mindrot.

C: Spores +12 vs. PD (1d3 nearby enemies)—20 damage and 5 ongoing poison damage (save ends).

Phosphorescent: The moss glows dimly. The first time it takes damage in a battle it lights up so brightly that it stuns (save ends) the nearest enemy that can see it.

Crawling horror: The moss can only move on rounds where the escalation die is odd. Whenever it takes holy damage it may immediately pop free of engagement and move as a free action.

Resist psychic 16+: When a psychic attack targets this creature, the attacker must roll a natural 16+ on the attack roll or it only deals half damage.

AC 23
PD 17   **HP 108**
MD 21

Mindrot

Those infected by mindrot slowly become hosts for the next generation of mindrot moss, helping to spread the infestation to new locations.

The disease starts at stage 1. At each full heal-up the target makes a DC 20 constitution check. A success moves the disease down one stage. A failure moves it up one stage.
 Stage 0: The target recovers from the disease.
 Stage 1: While affected by stage 1, the target takes a -2 penalty to MD.
 Stage 2: While affected by stage 2, the target's maximum hit points is reduced by half. Any creature that is engaged with the target at the start of its turn takes 5 poison damage.
 Stage 3: While affected by stage 3, the target becomes a mindrot thrall and will serve the moss... or will head toward a populated area, surviving for the next 2d4 days before it explodes in a mess of spores.

Mindrot Thrall

The half-corpses shamble forward, their eyes glowing from the moss that now fills their skulls.

Level 7 troop [PLANT]
Initiative: +8
Vulnerability: Fire

Mindless slam +12 vs. AC—20 damage

R: Acid spit +12 vs. PD—16 damage
 Natural 16+ hit or miss: 8 ongoing acid damage and target is stuck (save ends both).

C: Spore breath +12 vs. PD (1d3 nearby enemies)—16 damage, the target is weakened and takes 8 ongoing poison damage (save ends both).
 First Failed Save: In addition to the previous effects, the target contracts mindrot (stage 1).
 Limited use: Once per battle, recharges when staggered.

Fungal aura: When the mindrot thrall is reduced to below 50 hit points, all nearby creatures immediately take 8 poison damage.

Resist psychic 16+: When a psychic attack targets this creature, the attacker must roll a natural 16+ on the attack roll or it only deals half damage.

AC 23
PD 17   **HP 100**
MD 21

DEATH SWARM

Death butterflies and moths are sinister fey creatures that at first glance resemble harmless woodland insects. On closer inspection, the butterflies' dark wings give off a faint ghostly aura of negative energy. These spectral tendrils sap the life from creatures close to the swarm and feed the butterflies with the victim's energy.

INNOCENT-LOOKING GUARDIANS

Their deadly traits are well known among the fey, and some of the more malevolent feyborn lead lost travelers into areas where they know such swarms gather. Elven arcanists are rumored to have developed methods of mesmerizing the creatures, thus populating the gardens around their forest strongholds with butterfly swarms that serve as inconspicuous guardians against intruders.

THINGS YOU MIGHT FIND NEAR A DEATH SWARM...

A rose bush of surpassing beauty. Flowers, growing through the bones of an animal. The ruins of a cottage, now roofless and mostly covered in flowering ivy. A circle of trees, at the center of which is a dry well.

MAGIC ITEMS

The Diadem of Wings (crown/helm). A crown constructed to resemble a circle of glittering butterflies. *Recharge 18+:* Summon death butterflies to make an area impassable. If any living creature attempts to pass through the area they become stuck (save ends) and take 1d8 damage per round.

    Quirk: Surround yourself with flowers and corpses. Beautiful, beautiful flowers. Beautiful, beautiful corpses.

Lepidopteran Mask (mask/helm). A beautiful silk and lace half-mask made from the cocoon silk of a death moth or death butterfly. *Recharge 16+:* You and whatever equipment you're wearing transform into a swarm of fluttering rainbow moths or butterflies for up to one hour. While in this form you cannot be targeted by opportunity attacks, and may not attack or take any action except speaking or movement. (Your speech sounds like the whisper of fluttering wings.) Transforming into this form or back is a quick action. While in your swarm form you can fly, and may fit through any gap that a moth or butterfly could fit through.

    Quirk: Easily distracted.

ADVENTURE HOOKS

Deadly Vision: An aged star-gazing alseid has had a vision that a great event will begin at a certain spot at a certain time, and he will reward the party handsomely to convey him safely there. The locals call the spot "Little Death Wing Meadow."

Death Moth Swarm

The victim lies dead in his chamber, his once-fine clothes full of holes. From within the armoire you hear the fluttering of hundreds of tiny wings.

Level 7 swarm [BEAST]
Initiative: +16

Swarm of souleaters +12 vs. PD—20 damage and 8 ongoing negative energy damage (save ends).

C: Decaying embrace +12 vs. MD (1d3 nearby enemies)—20 damage and the target becomes confused (save ends). If the swarm or its target disengage, the target's saves against confused become easy saves.
Natural 16+ hit: The target cannot disengage from the swarm until it is destroyed.

Swarm resistance: The natural die result of any attack against this creature must be 11+ or it only does half damage. Close attacks or attacks than can target more than one enemy ignore this resistance, and instead do double damage on a hit or a miss.

Swarm dodge: Enemies cannot take opportunity attacks against the swarm, and enemies cannot pop free of engagement with the swarm nor cause the swarm to pop free. The swarm can fit through any gap that any member of the swarm can fit through.

Fluttering distraction: Nearby enemies take -2 to all saves.

Flight: The swarm can fly, though not in a high wind.

AC 25
PD 14   **HP 108**
MD 16

Death Butterfly Swarm

The cloud of butterflies swirls in the grove's dappled sunlight, the setting sun flashing on their black and white wings. As the cloud slowly moves deeper into the woods, it leaves behind the desiccated corpses of a half-dozen woodsmen.

Level 7 swarm [BEAST]
Initiative: +16

Swarm of souleaters +12 vs. PD—20 damage and 8 ongoing negative energy damage.

C: Weight of wings +12 vs. AC (1d2 nearby enemies)—28 damage
Natural 16+ hit or miss: Target is stuck (save ends).

Swarm attack: Once per round all nearby enemies takes 20 negative energy damage at the start of their turn.

Swarm resistance: The natural die result of any attack against this creature must be 11+ or it only does half damage. Close attacks or attacks than can target more than one enemy ignore this resistance and instead do double damage on a hit or a miss.

Swarm dodge: Enemies cannot take opportunity attacks against the swarm, and enemies cannot pop free of engagement with the swarm nor cause the swarm to pop free. The swarm can fit through any gap that any member of the swarm can fit through.

Flight: The swarm can fly, though not in a high wind.

AC 25
PD 14   **HP 108**
MD 16

Derro Fetal Savant

The derro are a malevolent race of dwarf-like creatures forced deep underground centuries ago.

They found a dark home—and equally dark gods to worship—in the subterranean realms beneath the Ironcrags. Here they nursed their hatreds and perfected the use of magics only whispered of in the sunlight.

SPREADING INSANITY

Only the most rare of derro are born with the rapidly fading ability to exchange souls with other creatures, and when discovered, the babbling infants are treated with bizarre and grotesque reverence. Placed in small, intricately wrought, pillowed cages and borne aloft on hooked golden staves, the wild-eyed newborns are carried standard-like behind battle lines to sow madness and confusion among enemy ranks.

CRAZED POSSESSORS

Fetal savants use their ability to randomly seize control of an appropriate victim among combatants to possess a host body; the savant attacks opponents wildly, relishing the physical power of the unfortunate host. Helpless without aid, a fetal savant greedily attempts to remain in a host body as long as possible. Its fate is otherwise in the hands of its bearer.

THINGS YOU MIGHT FIND WITH A DERRO FETAL SAVANT...

Silver chains. Silk pillow. Bottle of milk mixed with fresh blood. Cage, large enough to hold a tiny creature. Stave with a hook at the end (roll d4: 1= mostly gold with a steel core, 200gp worth. 2= gold-plated iron bands on wood, about 20gp worth. 3= gold-painted wood, worth about 5sp. 4= an ordinary 10' pole). Rattle full of tiny mouse bones. Leather swaddling clothes.

MAGIC ITEMS

Fetal Rattle (implement). A silver rod filled with tiny bones. *Once per day:* At the start of each of your turns, roll a d6. If you roll lower than the escalation die value then you may cast a daily spell that targets MD as a quick action on your turn. However, you may not use your standard action to cast a spell. *Quirk:* Claustrophobia.

ADVENTURE HOOKS

Dance of Madness: An embittered foe has secretly let the derro and their caged fetal savants into the city, where they skulk around gleefully causing havoc. Prominent citizens begin acting oddly: dancing, rending their clothes, and shouting obscenities.

The Mushroom War: The derro are capturing dwarven peasants and feeding them mushrooms that lower their ability to resist the commands of the fetal savants. The derro can now turn populations against themselves, sending brother against brother and friend against friend, all without risking themselves. The dwarves of the Ironcrags hire the adventurers to free their loved ones, burn whatever dank and fetid fungal cavern produces the mushrooms, and kill the derro.

Derro Savant Shrieker

These bizarre creatures act as living alarms. Once fetal savants, savant shriekers have outgrown their ability to possess a host. They simply hang in their cages in wall nooks to watch over derro halls, and alert their allies to the presence of intruders by loudly babbling and violently shaking the bars.

Level 3 spoiler [ABOMINATION]
Initiative: +7

C: Wail from the utter black +11 vs. MD (1d3 nearby enemies)—8 psychic damage and the target is weakened (save ends).

> *Natural 16+ hit or miss:* Make an additional attack as a free action against a second nearby creature (or the same creature if no others are nearby.)

C: Brainbleeder rebuke +11 vs. MD—10 psychic damage.

Psychobabble: Once the derro savant shrieker detects a nearby enemy it begins to babble and shriek loudly. Its cries attract any creature in the vicinity (nearby or far away) who cares to investigate.

Precious cargo: This creature can barely move on its own and must be carried by an ally. Picking up or putting down the savant shrieker is a quick action, but reduces the bearer's movement by half. (Treat nearby as far away for movement purposes.)

Resist psychic 16+: When a psychic attack targets this creature, the attacker must roll a natural 16+ on the attack roll or it only deals half damage.

Dominant mind: The derro cannot become confused.

AC 18
PD 14　　　**HP 7**
MD 19

Derro Fetal Savant

This creature appears to be a blue-skinned infant no older than a year. Its limbs flail, its head lolls with an obvious lack of coordination, and it screams incessantly. Of the madness that resonates so strongly in derro society, perhaps nothing is so twisted as fetal savants. These tiny, premature infants are born insane and destined to lead their people further into madness.

Level 10 spoiler [ABOMINATION]
Initiative: +7

C: Wail from the utter black +11 vs. MD (1d3 nearby enemies)—32 psychic damage and the target is weakened (save ends).

> *Natural 16+ hit or miss:* Make an additional attack as a free action against a second nearby creature (or the same creature if no others are nearby.)

C: Brainbleeder rebuke +11 vs. MD—58 psychic damage.

C: Despairing prison of flesh +15 vs. MD—23 psychic damage and the target is hampered (save ends).

On a failed save, or if the derro fetal savant makes a second successful *despairing prison of flesh* attack against a hampered foe, the target becomes confused (save ends) as the fetal savant controls their actions, forcing them to attack their allies. The derro fetal savant can only possess one foe at a time in this way, but makes the most of it.

Precious cargo: This creature can barely move on its own and must be carried by an ally. Picking up or putting down the fetal savant is a quick action, but reduces the bearer's movement by half. (Treat nearby as far away for movement purposes.)

Resist psychic 16+: When a psychic attack targets this creature, the attacker must roll a natural 16+ on the attack roll or it only deals half damage.

Dominant mind: The derro cannot become confused.

AC 26
PD 14　　　**HP 216**
MD 24

---

*Play up the horror of **despairing prison of flesh**—when the PC is hampered, describe how the warped, wretched, greedy mind of the derro fetal savant worms its way into their consciousness, weakening their willpower as it starts to seize control. If the fetal savant successfully possesses the PC, handle it as appropriate for your group: let the player act out being an insane psychic fetus in an adventurer's body, roleplay the fetal savant yourself while leaving the mechanics to the player, or let one or more other players dictate the PC's actions.*

Devils

The primary denizens of the Eleven Hells, devils are a strong and varied race. They live to serve the will of the archdevils and the dark gods who rule the Hells, or at least so it seems. Each devil, in truth, has designs to rule the Eleven Hells in its entirety.

DRIVEN BY PACTS

The devils of the Eleven Hells are some of the most lawful beings in Midgard. They might not think much of the laws of mortal rulers, but their own laws and pacts dictate much of their existence. The greatest of these laws come down from the lord of all devils, Asmodeus. Most regions of the Eleven Hells are ruled by an archdevil or dark god, who dictates the laws for their domain. Most mortals find these intricate and sometimes shifting rules fatally confusing, but the devils thrive on them.

Beyond the laws, devils live by pacts. Most often contracted between lesser and greater devils, these agreements enforce a hierarchy of power in the Hells. Devils often use imps and ink devils to assist in perfecting the wording of these pacts, as all sides seek to come out ahead. Of course, working with these devils means writing more contracts. Pacts with mortals are often much simpler, or at least the devil wants it to seem that way. In exchange for wealth or power, the mortal signs away its soul. However, the reward always comes with an additional price. Tainted by greed, madness, and a dark energy, contracting mortals rarely have the willpower to keep their own mind, and most soon become pawns of the infernal hierarchy.

MIDGARD'S DARK ENFORCERS

Sometimes mortals don't seek personal gain but powerful assistance. Devils contracted to other devils are often summoned into battle by mortals pledged to the devils' master, whether to aid a warlock engaged in an ancient ritual, protect a corrupted king, or perform some other service. Devils often appear for this reason among the gnomes of Niemheim. The price of such services is the same corruption that comes with pacts of power, only much worse.

Most summoners do not realize this. Many believe they have more control over the situation, but in reality, devils have far more influence when physically present because they get to oversee each step of the corruption themselves. Infinitely patient, they fine tune and twist each word and situation to drive the mortal's undoing. Once summoned, the devils gain access to their target's family, friends, and associates to sow the seeds of corruption among them all.

ADVENTURE HOOKS

Seventh Child: An ink devil claims that one of the adventurers owes it their soul, the result of a pact made by an ancestor in exchange for her true love being returned to life. That couple had a child, and that child had a child, and the adventurer is the seventh in line—so their soul is forfeit (unless they can provide seven times seven souls in their place). Is the devil telling the truth, or is there more at work here?

The Damned Forge: A foolish smith has made a deal with devils: fifty years of prosperity in exchange for his soul. As agreed, the devils have made the smith prosperous—by killing any other smith who sets up shop within two day's walk of his forge.

MASTERS OF SCROLL AND TOME, MINIONS OF TITIVILLUS

Ink devils are ranked among the lowest echelons of their kind, abused and tormented by all the greater devils. Twisted by the Archdevil Titivillus, they were once lemures and bearded devil scribes, bred and altered into extensions of his will. They work eternally grinding ink powders, formulating text and writing it out, and making copies of accounts, invoices, reports, bills, contracts, histories, works of praise to the archdevils, and pamphlets of slander or pure flattery. Ink devils live in libraries and scriptoria in the Hells and related planes. They serve any planar lord who wishes their help, and their speed and keen vision make them excellent accountants, recordkeepers, translators, and secretaries. They cannot be trusted, and their work is always confirmed by a second reader.

Ink devils are natural arcanists, and all can perform at least a few minor rituals. Those who find work as scribes in arcane libraries remember all they copy and soon find themselves powerful wizards in their own right. The brave might try to bargain with an ink devil for a performance or copy of a ritual, but the wise avoid such deals. Most words these creatures write are twisted in some manner. They have been known to give strangers a gift of letters of credit, or a charter, or scholarly papers, only for those papers to be found false, or even marked with explosive runes or other arcane traps.

Ink Devil

These lesser devils are deep black, with grey, inkstained, quill-like claws, shining white teeth, and red eyes. Their heads are often bald or fringed with hair in the style of a monastic haircut, and they have two small horns no larger than the tip of a thumb. They keep the books of Mammon's gold and mark the souls of sinners in each layer of the Hells. They also weigh the gains and losses in the struggles against chaos and against the angels. The scratching of their hundred thousand quills is the sound of Hell conspiring and taking through guile what it cannot win through force.

Level 2 troop [DEMON]
Initiative: +7

Inky claws +7 vs. AC—7 damage

C: Mark of evil +7 vs. MD (one nearby enemy)—Target becomes vulnerable to all attacks made by demons and devils (save ends).

The hidden word: Once per battle if there is a book or other text written in ink or paint nearby, the ink devil can roll a save. On a success it gains +4 to all defenses until the end of the battle.

[Special trigger] Disrupt concentration: When the ink devil is targeted by a ranged spell, as a free action it can give the spellcaster a -2 penalty to either the attack roll or the damage done. The use of this power is announced after the rolls to hit and damage have been made, and the results are known but before the results are applied.

Resist fire 11+: The natural die result of an attack against this creature involving fire must be 11+ or it only does half damage.

Teleport: The ink devil can teleport as a move action, disappearing in a swirl of ink to reappear at any point nearby that it can see.

AC 18
PD 14   **HP 36**
MD 14

TWISTED COGS AND REVISIONIST HISTORY

Hidden away in the private libraries of the Collegium Masters lies the true story of the birth of the gearforged. Before Zobeck's revolution, a brilliant and powerful arcanist called Kovacs experimented obsessively with various forms of artificial life. He refused to settle for the simple clockwork constructs of his day, and as he pursued a new form of true life, his experiments drifted very far from accepted practices. When the other masters finally ventured deep into his lab, what they found horrified them. Carcasses of animals, their vital organs replaced with mechanical parts, lay next to diabolic texts with obscene illustrations and blueprints calling for vitality harvested from sentient beings to power clockwork creatures.

While this mad research would grow into the foundation for the gearforged of today, these early, depraved prototypes were hunted by the Collegium and their allies. Some escaped to the Cartways and hidden crevices of the city. So the clockwork devils have survived, repairing themselves with the scraps from the geargrinders and steamworkers, all while gathering cultists to their side. Rumors say that some of Kovacs' notes went unaccounted for, leaving the possibility for others of grave ambitions to follow his infernal path.

Clockwork Devil

At first glance, the creatures rising from the shadows resemble some infernal beings, but a closer look reveals whirring gears, cogs, and cables binding their joints together. The glowing crimson eyes and brimstone scents of these clockwork constructs confirms their infernal natures, however.

Clockwork devils know nothing of fear, only duty and programming. Built from gears, cogs, and metal casing like other clockwork, these abominations are twisted into visions from the Eleven Hells. The ritual to complete their creation pulls infernal essence up into the world to create a truly evil metal beast.

Large level 3 troop [DEMON/CONSTRUCT]
Initiative: +9

Slam +8 vs. AC—21 damage
  Natural 16+ hit or miss: Infernal breath recharges.

[Special trigger] **C: Clockwork surprise +8 vs. AC (one nearby enemy)**—10 damage
  Usable once per round against a nearby enemy who uses a move action to move, or when a far away enemy uses a move action to move nearby.

C: Infernal breath +9 vs. PD (one nearby enemy)—45 fire damage
  Limited use: Once per battle, but may be used again if the devil rolls 16+ on a slam or when it is staggered.

Infernal power: When the devil is reduced to 0 hit points or below it immediately makes three *infernal breath* attacks as free actions.

Resist cold and fire 11+: When a cold or fire attack targets this creature, the attacker must roll a natural 11+ on the attack roll or it only deals half damage.

AC 19
PD 16   **HP 90**
MD 14

LAST TO THE FIGHT

Rarely seen in their natural form outside of Hell, gilded devils are the favored servants of Mammon, archdevil of greed. They tempt and corrupt with promises of wealth, power, and fame, twisting mortal greed into unforgivable damnation. Gilded devils prefer unassuming appearances. They mold their flesh and adopt gaudy trappings to look the parts of wise advisers, canny merchants, or sly confidants.

Gilded devils disdain direct combat, preferring to leave battle to manipulated mortals or loyal thralls. If forced to fight, however, the devil typically attempts to trap enemies in pools of molten gold before stealing the belongings of others and leaving. A coward at heart, a gilded devil will flee if pressed and assume a new form to facilitate its escape.

Gilded Devil

This tall and bronze-complexioned man is abnormally long-limbed and clad in armor of stained and battered coins. His wiry frame is festooned with mismatched and gaudy bracelets, rings, and necklaces. He licks his lips as his eyes take inventory of your possessions.

Level 3 spoiler [DEMON]
Initiative: +9

Scourge of avarice +8 vs. AC—10 damage
  Natural 20+: Amass all things triggered.

R: Betrayal of riches +8 vs. PD—10 damage and roll a d4
  1. If the target is wearing magic bracers or gloves it becomes dazed (save ends); if not, the target becomes confused (save ends).
  2. If the target is wearing magic boots or shoes it becomes stuck (save ends); if not, the target becomes confused (save ends).
  3. If the target is wearing a magical ring it becomes weakened (save ends); if not, the target becomes confused (save ends).
  4. If the target is wearing a magic helm or hat it becomes confused (save ends); if not, the target becomes confused (hard save ends).
  Natural 20+: Amass all things triggered.

R: The wealth beneath your feet +8 vs. PD (1d3 nearby enemies)—10 damage and target is stuck (save ends).
  Miss: 5 damage.
  Natural 20+: Amass all things triggered.

[Special trigger] Amass all things: As a single free action the gilded devil teleports the target's most valuable item into its grasp, teleports itself somewhere nearby, and then runs away from the battle with its prize.

Greed's many forms: The gilded devil may alter its physical form to appear to be any medium or small humanoid, and may shift its form at will. It resumes its normal form if it is reduced to 0 hit points or below. Other creatures can make a DC 35 wisdom check to see through the disguise. A result of 30-34 will at least allow the one making the check to notice that it is a disguise.

Resist fire 11+: When a fire attack targets this creature, the attacker must roll a natural 11+ on the attack roll or it only deals half damage.

AC 19
PD 13   **HP 40**
MD 17

ENGINES OF INFERNAL COMBUSTION

There is a corner of Hell known simply as the Forge. Here, black chimneys rise a mile above a dead land of choking air and red poison hills. The Machine, a greater devil who never sleeps and gives his subjects no rest, rules this land. His overseers consist of thousands upon thousands of imps who whip and punish the workers. The imps themselves are kept in check by hordes of chain devils, who in turn answer to the automata—the managers of this infernal place. Automata devils are chain devils who have been granted this special reward.

Automata devils are part devil and part living machine. The machine part knows only that toil must never end, and they are merciless in their judgment, wanting only for the Forge to continue. The devil part comes in when punishments need to be created or modified. Automata devils live to dominate, especially in petty, purely physical ways. Their role is to monitor others, and they regularly have charge of prisoners or infernal factories.

Automata Devil (Castigas)

Infernal machines are true horrors to behold. Legends tell not just of their size and tortuous ends, but of the living cogs that keep them running. This slender, almost emaciated, creature's skin erupts in barbs, sharp nails, and coils of wire threaded through its flesh. Chains lie buried under blisters and scabs. The eyelids— both front and back pairs—have been sewn back with wire, while six arms ending in large grasping hands erupt from its shoulders.

Large level 6 troop [CONSTRUCT/DEMON]
Initiative: +12

C: **Whip +11 vs. PD (1 nearby enemy)**—36 damage and the devil can drag the target into engagement (target is grabbed). On the devil's next turn, if the target is still grabbed the devil makes a *punishing embrace* attack against the target. The devil can only grab one enemy at a time with its whip, but feeding a target into its maw frees the whip for another grab attempt.

[Special trigger] **Punishing embrace +15 vs. PD (1 creature grabbed by the automata devil's' whip)**—42 damage and the target is stunned (save ends) as the devil throws the target into its stomach maw, a mass of churning gears with serrated edges, clockwork gears, and whirling blades. The +4 bonus against grabbed foes is already added to the attack roll.

Lacerate: The automata devil can make six *whip* attacks. Any creature hit by two or more attacks is dazed (save ends).
Limited use: Once per battle.

Fear aura: Enemies engaged with the automata devil and who have 30 hit points or less are dazed and can't use the escalation die.

AC 22
PD 20   **HP 180**
MD 19

DOGMOLE

The Ironcrag dwarves have domesticated many subterranean creatures including a breed of giant *talpidae* commonly called dogmoles. Energetic and obedient, dogmoles pull ore-trolleys through mines, sniff out toxic gases and polluted waters, and help dig out trapped miners. Their uncanny ability to detect imminent cave-ins and burrowing monsters makes them welcome companions in the depths. Outside the mines, dogmoles serve as pack animals, guards, and bloodhounds. Derro also keep dogmoles, but the creatures are scarred and brutalized savages, barely controllable even by their handlers.

LOYAL PROTECTORS

Not normally aggressive, dogmoles warn off most enemies with a rumbling growl, though they often attack large invertebrates immediately. Dogmoles begin combat with a charge and snap at foes with their long incisors. They typically retreat if seriously injured, but will fight to the death to protect their pack, their young, or their dwarven masters. Dogmoles cannot burrow into solid rock, but they can move through softer material like soil or loose rubble, leaving a usable 5-foot diameter tunnel.

THINGS YOU MIGHT FIND WITH A DOGMOLE…

Collar with a short length of chain attached to it. Collar with a frayed rope attached to it. Much-chewed bone. Bandanna around its neck—perhaps an ordinary piece of cloth, or perhaps something more important that the dogmole's master didn't recognize.

MAGIC ITEMS

Dogmole Pipe (wondrous item). Carved from a dogmole's thigh bone, this pipe is a favorite of wizards. While the wizard smokes the pipe it confers a +4 bonus to ritual casting checks, provided the ritual involves stones, dirt, or tunnels.

Recharge 6+: When not in combat you may burrow through the earth (but not through stone) for five minutes.

Quirk: You prefer to rest in the dirt.

ADVENTURE HOOKS

Molecoach: A wagon-master has become obsessed with the idea of dogmole-pulled wagons. They will be able to travel overland and underground; and while dogmoles are not as fast as horses, they are far smarter. He needs protection travelling to the Ironcrags with a large sum of gold, and help with bringing his new pack of dogmoles back home. Are the adventurers willing to help him out? They'll be paid for each dogmole that safely makes it.

Unquiet Corpse: A restless spirit cannot find peace until its remains are given a proper burial. Unfortunately, its mortal form was killed by derro and its remains have been made into armor for a dogmole juggernaut.

Dogmole

This mole-like creature is the size of a large dog, but its thick, barrel-shaped body looks as heavy as a full-grown dwarf. A ring of tentacles sprouts above its mouth, which is dominated by spade-like incisors. Despite lacking visible ears and possessing only tiny, cataract-filled eyes, it clearly senses its environment.

Large level 2 troop [BEAST]
Initiative: +7

Gouging teeth +7 vs. AC—14 damage
 Miss: 7 damage.

Tenacious rage: When first staggered the dogmole can make a *gouging teeth* attack as an immediate free action, and it gains +2 to all defenses until the end of its next turn.

Scent: The dogmole is almost completely blind; it uses scent to detect nearby creatures, even those who are invisible. Dogmoles make great watchdogs.

Subterranean burrower: A dogmole can burrow swiftly through soil and rubble.

AC 18
PD 16   **HP 70**
MD 12

Dogmole Juggernaut

What the derro have done with certain breeds of dogmole almost defies description. Brutalized from birth and hardened by scarification, foul drugs, and unnatural magics, the dogmole juggernaut is barely recognizable as a relative of its smaller kin. A furless mass of muscle, scar tissue, and barbed piercings clad in haphazard barding, it stands 7 feet at the shoulder and 9 to 12 feet long. Its incisors are the length of short swords. The derro use these warped dogmoles as mounts and improvised siege engines. When not at war, the derro enjoy pitting juggernauts against one another in frenzied gladiatorial combats.

Triple strength level 3 wrecker [BEAST]
Initiative: +3

Gouging teeth +8 vs. AC—30 damage
   Miss: 15 damage.
   Ferocious charge: The attack instead deals 40 damage on a hit if the dogmole juggernaut first moves before attacking an enemy it was not engaged with at the start of its turn.

Rapid rebuke: When a dogmole juggernaut is hit by a melee attack it may immediately make a *gouging teeth* attack against the one who hit it as a quick action.

Murderous frenzy: The first time in a battle that the dogmole juggernaut reduces an enemy to 0 hit points or less, it may make an extra attack on its next turn as a free action. If the extra attack is a natural even roll, the dogmole may make another extra attack on its next turn as a quick action.

Scent: The dogmole is almost completely blind; it uses scent to detect nearby creatures, even those who are invisible. Dogmoles make great watchdogs.

Subterranean burrower: A dogmole can burrow swiftly through soil and rubble.

Nastier Specials:
Regeneration: While a dogmole juggernaut is damaged, it heals 10 hit points at the start of its turn. It can regenerate five times per battle. If it heals to its maximum hit points, then that use of regeneration doesn't count against the five-use limit. Dropping a dogmole juggernaut to 0 hit points doesn't kill it if it has any uses of *regeneration* left.

AC 19
PD 17   **HP 135**
MD 13

DRAKE

Midgard scholars acknowledge the pseudodragon as the first true drake. The creatures regularly appeared to travelers over the centuries, somehow finding the one person worthy of aid among any group. In time, arcane spellcasters realized the value of these creatures as companions, leading to their proliferation.

Other pseudodragons settled in large cities like Zobeck and served the same role as cats—though they tended to eliminate more powerful nuisances such as gremlins, imps, and even the stray goblin or kobold.

PROUD FAMILIARS, MANY VARIETIES

As pseudodragons spread, people initially referred to them as "common drakes" (pseudodragons naturally rejected any notion of being "common"). Those arcane spellcasters who took to the creatures called them "familiar drakes," while households graced by their presence named them "house drakes."

Other drakes appeared once pseudodragons became a common sight, almost as if they had heralded the arrival of a completely new species. It seems as though explorers and scholars discover new drakes every year, each apparently tied to some common theme from geographical features to important materials or even abstract ideas. While plenty of drakes have been studied and classified, many remain a mystery other than their "theme."

ADVENTURE HOOKS

The Drakes of Wrath: A trouble-making alehouse drake has taken up residence in a tavern, taking petty revenge on the tavern-keeper every time she tries to dislodge the trickster from the rafters. She will give the adventurers free drinks for a year if they can get rid of the pest. But the tavern regulars have taken a liking to the creature and will react poorly to any attempts to get rid of it.

The Best Laid Plans of Drakes and Men: Twin sisters have unknowingly married the same man, a confidence trickster who enlisted the aid of a different pact drake for each wedding. Both pact drakes insist that the marriage they presided over is valid and the other one invalid—a situation that will allow the groom to seize control of both sisters' assets. The sisters are refusing to cooperate with the drakes, who are being driven mad trying to work out the ins and outs of their conflicting pacts. Can the adventurers sort things out?

ALEHOUSE DRAKE

Alehouse drakes average about 18 inches long and weigh about 18 pounds with a plump belly. Their scales tend toward deep amber with cream or white highlights, and they possess glittering, light-colored eyes. Their breath weapon is an intoxicating cloud of stale beer fumes. The mischievous alehouse drake appears mostly in the central and northern regions of Midgard. Large cities in the domains of Dornig, Krakova, and Magdar typically have at least one such creature. Even across the Neider Strait in Trollheim, alehouse drakes sometimes choose a drinking hall to champion, though their more whimsical cousins consider these dour drakes far too serious.

Mostly a nuisance, alehouse drakes squat in bars, taverns, and inns, the busier the better. A bane or savior to every bartender and innkeeper, alehouse drakes enjoy pushing patrons' emotions to ecstatic cheers or bloody bar fights. Alehouse drakes prefer escape to confrontation but are ornery when cornered.

FUN-LOVING TAVERN-DWELLERS

Alehouse drakes typically make their homes in busy and populated cities and towns, but as they age, they prefer to escape the hustle and bustle and lair in roadside coaching inns and more isolated taverns. In the former situations, alehouse drakes are often troublemakers or pranksters, but in the latter circumstances, they usually befriend the proprietor and help manage flared tempers and weepy drinkers in return for living space and a generous tab.

INCORRIGIBLE GOSSIPS

Easily one of the most talkative types of drake, alehouse drakes gossip endlessly. They pick up a lot of stories while perched in hiding places throughout a busy tavern, and many trade in information. An alehouse drake can serve as a good source for goings on about town, especially events occurring in their establishment. More devious and ill-mannered alehouse drakes resort to blackmail, but usually only to secure a comfortable spot in their chosen tavern.

An odd, one-sided rivalry has sprung up between alehouse drakes and pact drakes, with the former trying in vain to get the latter to loosen up. For their part, pact drakes mostly ignore the cajoling and puerile taunts, but overly persistent alehouse drakes sometimes find their chosen home shut down due to obscure ordinance violations.

ERSTWHILE INNKEEPERS

Alehouse drakes prefer acting alone, but sometimes as they age, they take mates and live a coupled life. In particularly large and cosmopolitan cities, a revel of alehouse drakes might control all the inns, tap houses, and other drinking establishments in an entire district, shifting patrons' emotions for fun or profit. The oldest recorded alehouse drake—the light-hearted Essammith—lived just past 400 years, inhabiting the same tavern for most of that period.

Alehouse Drake

This plump little creature reclines lazily in the tavern's rafters, a dazed look in its eyes and the suggestion of a grin on its fanged jaws

Level 1 spoiler [DRAGON]
Initiative: +3

Claw and bite +6 vs. AC—5 damage
   Natural 16+ hit: Discombobulating is triggered.

C: Beery breath +6 vs. PD (1d3 nearby targets)—5 damage and the target is stuck (save ends)
   Natural 16+ hit: Discombobulating is triggered.
   Failed save against stuck: Target is stuck and hampered (save ends both).
   Failed save against stuck and hampered: Target is helpless (save ends all conditions, even those not from *beery breath*).

Discombobulating: The alehouse drake becomes invisible until the end of its next turn (+5 to all defenses) and makes the following attack:

Alehouse discombobulation +6 vs. MD—target is dazed until the end of the drake's next turn and forgets the events of the battle once it is over.

Flight: The drake can fly, weaving through the air almost as if it were drunk.

AC 17
PD 11   **HP 27**
MD 15

CRAG DRAKE

Crag drakes are the one drake that dwarves truly fear, for in addition to their powerful bite and stony claws, they have a caustic breath that allows them to literally eat gold and other ores.

A crag drake's coloration and stealthy nature help disguise it in darkened mine shafts and natural caverns. It stands between 5 and 6 feet tall at the shoulder and nearly 15 feet long from flickering tongue to whipping tail. Powerful muscles, a compact build, and a dense, rocky hide contribute to its roughly 1,200 pound weight. Crag drakes prefer to hunt alone, but several individuals may share especially rich hunting grounds. A crag drake, as a creature of stone, finds comfort in the cramped bowels of the earth. A forbidding mountain and yawning black tunnels, the glitter of ore just below the surface, and the hiss of gases seeping through slow-splitting fissures are the hallmarks of home for these prowling fiends.

HUNTERS DEEP BELOW

The bane of successful mining operations, crag drakes stalk underground denizens to consume both them and their precious minerals. These stealthy and cunning beasts often lie in wait for days to ambush prospective miners and underground wanderers with corrosive breath, vicious teeth and claws, and elusive cunning. Despite this, because they always appear near rich veins of metals or minerals, some prospectors consider the presence of a crag drake a sign of good luck.

GREEDY ROCK EATERS

Crag drakes can blossom like dangerous parasites in any mountain range. In central Midgard, these nefarious creatures most often appear in the Ironcrag and Cloudwall Mountains. To the east, the population of crag drakes surges in the Dragoncoil Mountains, adding to the dangers of that massive range.

Crag Drake

This creature's powerful limbs end in jagged metallic talons, and chipped stone teeth line its powerful jaws. Rocky protrusions mark its durable hide, and its serpentine tail lashes wickedly.

Level 4 troop [DRAGON]
Initiative: +9

Claw and bite +9 vs. AC—14 damage
Natural even hit: 5 ongoing acid damage.
Natural odd hit or miss: Corrosive breath recharges.

C: Corrosive breath +14 vs. AC (1d3 nearby enemies)—14 damage and 5 ongoing acid damage
Miss: 7 damage.

Spry dash: The crag drake make disengage with an easy (6+) check if it is standing on stone, concrete, or rubble.

Earthwalk: The drake can climb over walls and along ceilings as quickly as it can move along the ground, and can run over rubble and broken stone as fast as though it were going over flat ground.

Earthsense: Provided it is in contact with bare dirt or stone, the drake can sense everything nearby and far away that is in contact with the stone.

Stone meld: The drake may meld with a stone wall or floor that it is in contact with as a move action. While melded the drake is difficult to harm (it gains resist all damage 16+) and regenerates 5 hit points at the start of each of its turns. The drake can only dimly perceive the world while melded, but can "swim" through the stone as a move action. If the drake moves away from the stone or attacks, the meld ends immediately.

AC 20
PD 18 **HP 54**
MD 14

GEAR DRAKE

Gear drakes are stout and dense for their size, stretching just over 5 feet from nose to tail but often weighing 150 pounds. Rare even by drake standards, gear drakes nest near industries and areas of technological innovation, making them intrinsically associated with Zobeck. Even the creatures themselves claim to originate in that city, though a few gear drakes make their home in the Sultanate. Haughty gear drakes claim credit for the birth of industry and invention in Zobeck—their "gift of gears" to mankind—though historians disagree.

Skilled with all manner of tools and machines, a gear drake can serve as a trusted workmate or a spiteful saboteur. They represent the ingenuity of craftsmanship, and many tradesmen regard having one roost in their workshop as highly prestigious. A gear drake doesn't lend its services to just anyone. These proud and particular creatures only work with those who share their work ethic and perfectionism.

MACHINE-LIKE APPEARANCE

Gear drakes possess a strange physiology. Their bones have the texture of polished metal, their joints a mechanical precision, and their bodies a machined appearance. Stripped of flesh, they resemble a complex construct more than a natural creature. Their scales have a metallic hue and odd bumps that resemble rivets. Despite this, they are indeed creatures of flesh and blood.

DEMANDING PARTNERS

Gear drakes see other drakes as components in the world's great machine and maintain friendly relationships with them. They especially enjoy the company of steam drakes, who often inhabit the same workshops and forges, but also work well with other types. Gear drakes often draft elaborate plans requiring the assistance of paper, glass, and even ash drakes. They make it very clear that they control the project, however, and hold their cousins to their own high standards, generally making such partnerships short affairs.

By contrast, gear drakes will often work with each other for years, particularly on large-scale projects. The relationships that grow from these projects often lead to a new great endeavor: the next generation of gear drakes. The clutch of 2–4 eggs takes about a month to gestate and almost a year to hatch. Each parent then spends another year teaching the hatchlings and tinkering to ensure the best possible advantages for their offspring. After a year, the young drakes leave to find their own way.

TWISTED MINORITY

While most gear drakes love to create, some malign gear drakes live to break everything around them. These vile creatures stalk and ambush gearforged in back alleys, wreck workshops, or burn laboratories. Evil gear drakes sometimes serve spiteful inventors, taking bribes to destroy a competitor's facilities and tools.

Gear Drake

Like a sleek machine made flesh, this draconic creature moves with smooth, well-oiled precision. Its scales seem to sweat a thin film of grease on everything it touches.

Level 3 troop [DRAGON]
Initiative: +5

Claw and bite +8 vs. AC—10 damage
  Natural 1-5: Cacophonous breath recharges.
  Natural 18+ hit: One tiny non-magical item on the target's person shatters.

R: Telekinetic strike +8 vs. PD—10 damage
  Natural 1-5: Cacophonous breath recharges.
  Natural 16+ hit or miss: The target becomes stuck (save ends).

C: Cacophonous breath +8 vs. PD (1d3 nearby enemies)—10 thunder damage and the target is weakened (hard save ends)
  Miss: 5 thunder damage.
  Limited use: This ability may only be used once per battle, but it recharges and may be used again if another attack made by the drake is a natural 1-5 roll.

Flight: The drake can fly - its wings flap rapidly and mechanically.

Watchful: The drake does not sleep, and is immune to potions or spells that attempt to make it sleep.

Resist fire 16+: When a fire attack targets this creature, the attacker must roll a natural 16+ on the attack roll or it only deals half damage.

Craftsdrake: The drake can mend objects (treat as a *mending* cantrip).

AC 19
PD 13   **HP 45**
MD 15

PACT DRAKE

While its 4-foot long body and 1-foot long tail make a pact drake seem insignificant, it carries an unmistakable presence in any hall of power. The creatures sometimes take on affectations to further their image, usually a mantle, miter, chain, or some other symbol of office or authority.

The draconic embodiment of Law, a pact drake makes its home in large cities or other seats of authority. They often appear at major negotiations, as if drawn by an uncanny sense. Sometimes welcomed, sometimes not, the drakes nevertheless ensure that all parties honor the contract.

Some nations or powerful individuals retain the services of a pact drake, usually by providing historical, legal, or religious documents. Some of these creatures also demand trivial payment in gems and jewels; though trivial to the drake could mean up to 10% of the kingdom's treasure. Delicate negotiations between rival humanoid powers sometimes fall to the pact drakes employed by both sides.

BOUND BY ITS COVENANTS

A pact drake must enforce all deals it brokers. If for any reason it cannot enforce a deal, the drake suffers -4 to attack rolls, saves, and ability and skill checks. This condition can only be lifted by enforcing the deal, by a magical ritual performed by an epic tier spellcaster, or by another pact drake convinced the afflicted drake has atoned. Pact drakes understand this and work to handle every contract meticulously. Pact drakes can check on those who have entered into a pact by concentrating on the subject—this conjures a 'scrying eye' in the creature's location through which the pack can observe goings-on.

MUTUAL RESPECT

Courtship for a pact drake is simply another sort of negotiation. The two drakes meet, determine which drake will raise the young, how much assistance or compensation the other drake will provide, agree to terms, and finally consummate the deal. The union typically results in a small brood of 2-4 drakes—some sages humorously suggest the pair negotiate the number of young along with all other terms. Pact drakes reside in cities where law and regulations flourish, acting as overseers and mediators. A handful of pact drakes hail from Niemheim, where they act as companions to the pact-making gnomes who call those lands home.

Pact Drake

This small draconic creature holds itself with the poise of a learned scholar or a righteous judge. Discerning eyes peer past a scaled snout and toothy jaws.

Level 5 troop [DRAGON]
Initiative: +12

Claw and Bite +13 vs. AC—18 damage

C: Punish transgressors +13 vs. MD (1d3 nearby creatures)—18 damage and the target is dazed (save ends). If the target has broken a pact brokered by the drake, the target takes an additional 9 damage if this attack hits.

Transgressor-pacifying breath +13 vs. MD (all nearby creatures,)— The target is calmed and cannot make attacks or deal damage (treat as stunned, save ends). If the target has broken a pact brokered by the drake, the target also takes 21

damage if this attack hits. Any further damage to or attacks against the target ends the stunned condition.

Cunning mind: The pact drake is a natural linguist and becomes fluent in any language after just a short while studying it, sometimes learning a new language after just minutes of exposure to it being spoken.

True vision: The pact drake is immune to illusions. Invisibility and the spell *blur* do not work on a pact drake.

Magical flight: The pact drake can fly gracefully, and once per battle can teleport while in flight. The teleportation is a free action and can take the drake to any point nearby that it can see.

AC 21	
PD 16	**HP 50**
MD 18	

STEAM DRAKE

Steam drakes measure just over 5 feet from nose to tail but weigh less than 30 pounds. Their lusterless scales vary in shade from white to pale gray. Though rare, steam drakes make their homes in bustling cities renowned for technical research and knowledge.

Steam drakes admire the industry of dwarves, kobolds, and humans and often assist in the research and design of mechanical devices. Just over a dozen steam drakes inhabit the Free City of Zobeck, mainly in the Gear District, and perhaps as many roost throughout the Ironcrag Cantons. Steam drakes have a sometimes-contentious relationship with gear drakes. While some work well with gear drakes, others are haughty and outright hostile to their mechanically inclined kin.

A rare few steam drakes have a more bestial and raw outlook. These savage steam drakes live near underground gas vents, secluded hot springs, or even steaming fissures in mountains, growing larger and feral in their isolation.

DRAKE-POWERED MACHINERY

Steam drakes sometimes consent to serve as an energy source for their creations. In its steam form, the drake can pulse through devices designed for steam power and bring the machine to action. This requires an immense sense of trust and sublimation and thus occurs quite rarely.

An excited or startled steam drake emits a shrill whistle, varying in tone depending on the drake's emotion, to frighten off any threats or alert others to danger or an interesting discovery.

Steam drakes actually need an abundant source of steam to survive. They seem to draw sustenance from inhaling and immersing themselves in the super-heated vapor. They supplement this with a diet of rodents scalded to death before the drake consumes them.

HOT AND STEAMY

Steam drakes prefer to reproduce in natural hot springs or constantly running foundries. In steam form each drake commingles with the other drake. This quickly results in droplets of condensation—actually 4–8 eggs mixed with moisture—that fall near the hottest portion of the venting. Both parents raise the young, which mature in 15 months.

Steam Drake

The air shimmers with heat distortion around this small draconic creature. Quick and lithe, the beast flies through the air with exceptional ease.

Level 6 troop [DRAGON]
Initiative: +13
Vulnerable: cold

Claw and bite +14 vs. AC—21 damage

C: Scalding breath +14 vs. PD (1d3 nearby enemies)—21 fire damage
Miss: 10 damage.
Limited use: Scalding breath can be used once per battle, unless it recharges.

Steam form: The drake can transform itself into living steam, moving through keyholes and cracks or drifting through the air. In this form it may not make attacks apart from *scald*, but its movement doesn't provoke attacks and it may move as a quick action. Transforming to and from this form is a quick action.

C: Scald +14 vs. PD (one nearby enemy)—14 fire damage
Natural 16+: scalding breath recharges.

Flight: The steam drake can fly expertly, and if flying can choose to make its attack mid-move; continuing the movement after the attack does not provoke.

Dark vision: The drake can see perfectly well in even the most lightless environs.

Watchful: The drake does not sleep and is immune to potions or spells that attempt to make it sleep.

Resist fire 16+: When a fire attack targets this creature, the attacker must roll a natural 16+ on the attack roll or it only deals half damage.

AC 22
PD 20   **HP 65**
MD 16

FELLFORGED

Fellforged are clockwork creatures given foul sentience when their bodies—specially constructed to house the spirits of the dead—come into contact with deathshade wisps who yearn to wreak havoc on the corporeal world. Containing the wisps in these constructs dulls many of their supernatural abilities, but gives their terrible anger a physical form. They twist this form to their own use, even going so far as to destroy the body in their attempts to harm the living.

ANCESTRAL SERVITORS

Every kingdom has its royal guards, stoic souls with vigilant eyes, strong arms, and unmatched loyalty. The Courts of the Shadow Fey are no different. However, the desire for that precious final quality—loyalty—has forced its nobles to seek unorthodox guardians. Knowing that no living shadow fey could fully set aside its own ambition, the court turned to its ancestors. Cemeteries were pillaged and corpses exhumed. Spirits were pulled from the shadows. This fusing of necromancy and shadow essence culminated in the deathshade wisp. These gaunt, wraith-like warriors now stalk the kingdom, bound to serve the court and unflagging in their duty. They can even rise to rule part of the realm themselves, given enough time.

RELENTLESS ATTACKERS

Deathshade wisps who become fellforged hate life, and fight until destroyed. They have little regard for the bodies they inhabit or those of their fellows, and they do not hold back. When injured, they aim to catch as many opponents as possible in their scornful gearblast and may even set off a chain reaction among their allies if fighting close to other fellforged.

All animals, whether wild or domesticated, can sense the unnatural presence of fellforged and will not to go near them unless forced to do so. Fellforged communicate with each other in harsh, metallic voices.

ADVENTURE HOOKS

The Fantastic Doll: When an old jar in a junk shop falls and shatters, the deathshade wisps magically trapped in it escape into a set of antique clockwork dolls. In their weakened state these newly-created fellforged cannot leave the shop—but feeding on the lives of a party of adventurers would give them the strength to depart and find more suitable containers. The owner (who has been convinced that the spirits in the dolls are trapped heroes in need of help) entices the party to visit his establishment with hints of a mysterious item for sale.

The Fell Flood: A huge fellforged of incredible power lies buried and dormant beneath a village—and the fellforged are determined to unleash it on the world again. They plan to sweep the entire town away by destroying a nearby dam.

Fellforged

This brass automaton resembles a gearforged, but a vaguely disturbing angularity in its face and a darkly intelligent glow its eyes give it an infernal cast.

Level 5 spoiler [CONSTRUCT/UNDEAD]
Initiative: +9

Deathslam +10 vs. AC—18 negative energy damage

C: Lifedrinker strike +10 vs. PD (one nearby enemy)—18 damage, 5 ongoing negative energy damage (save ends) and the target pops free.
Natural even hit: The fellforged makes an *unnatural resonance* attack against the target as a quick action.

C: Unnatural resonance +10 vs. MD (one nearby enemy)—10 psychic damage and the target is stunned (save ends).

Hellish gears: When the fellforged is reduced to 37 hit points or less it makes a *scornful gearblast* attack; and once again when the fellforged is reduced to 0 hit points or less.

[Special trigger] **C: Scornful gearblast +10 vs. PD (1d3 nearby enemies)**—18 damage, 5 ongoing negative energy damage (save ends) and the target pops free.

Resist poison, negative energy, holy 16+: When an attack with the listed damage types targets this creature, the attacker must roll a natural 16+ on the attack roll or it only deals half damage.

Immune to sleep: Spells or effects that cause sleep do not affect the fellforged.

AC 21
PD 20   **HP 74**
MD 15

Deathshade Wisp

A ball of light forms into the lanky, pallid shape of a shadow fey with rotting skin.

Level 7 troop [UNDEAD]
Initiative: +13
Vulnerable: holy

Shadow spear +12 vs. AC—28 damage

C: Death's journey +12 vs. AC (1d3 nearby enemies)—10 damage as the wisp teleports around the battlefield striking at multiple foes, returning in an eyeblink to where it began.

Shadow step: As a standard action the wisp teleports to any nearby foe and makes the following melee attack:

Grave-calling stab +12 vs. AC—14 damage and the target is stuck (save ends)
  Natural 16+ hit or miss: The wisp uses *shadow step* again as a free action.

Insubstantial: This creature has resist damage 16+ to all damage types except force and holy damage, which damage it normally. If the wisp takes holy damage it loses this ability until the start of its next turn.

Flight: The wisp can hover above the ground, drifting through the air light as a silk shroud or darting about like a wasp. The wisp rarely moves more than a foot off the ground, its feet trailing along behind it.

[Special trigger] Fading light: When the wisp is reduced to 50 hit points or less it immediately teleports to any place nearby or far away that it can see.

AC 23
PD 16   **HP 100**
MD 17

GHOST BOAR OF THE RINGWOOD

Legend says that the ghost boars of the Ringwood were once simply dire boars—big, fierce, and wild, but still natural creatures. The elves and humans of the Valeran Empire hunted them for sport and food, and sometimes tamed them for use in battle. In the chaotic wars following the Great Retreat, a great white boar gave its life to rescue St. Gerita of the Grey Cowl, a priestess of Charon the Boatman, when raiders from Capleon attacked her. For that service, supposedly, the God of Death blessed the boars of the Ringwood with fell magical powers.

AGGRESSIVE COMBATANTS

Whatever the truth, ghost boars are dangerous animals, wandering the forest in small groups and attacking those who stray into their territory. Travelers in Kammae Straboli sometimes say that the boars only attack outsiders, particularly those from the rival cities of Capleon and Valera, but this seems unlikely. A boar will typically charge straight at the middle of a group, attempting to knock the biggest opponent down, and then turn insubstantial. Ghost boars are known to stomp upon the ground to cause shadowy tendrils to rise and rend opponents.

SERVANTS OF THE BOATMAN

A mysterious group of holy warriors belonging to the Order of St. Gerita make their home in a small monastery hidden deep in the Ringwood. These holy warriors unswervingly serve Charon the Boatman, dedicating their lives to hunting down the undead wherever they appear and laying them to rest. The order has trained a number of ghost boars to serve as its protectors. The inquisitors of Kammae Straboli are naturally very keen to question anyone who has come across these trained boars and their handlers.

THINGS YOU MIGHT FIND ON A GHOST BOAR…

Nothing, it's a boar. Unless maybe it's a torn scrap of cloth caught on one of the ghost boar's tusks, which will prove to be a vital clue that unlocks a world-changing mystery… but probably not.

MAGIC ITEMS

Ghost Armor (armor, any type). This armor made of leather and bone from a ghost boar seems to phase in and out of reality.

Recharge 11+: The first time in a battle that you take damage you may teleport to any point nearby as a quick action.

Quirk: Your flesh is ghost-like and translucent in places.

ADVENTURE HOOKS

Pilgrimage to the Ringwood: A young woman asks the party to accompany her on her annual journey into the Ringwood, where her family was killed and buried. She says she's seen in a vision that this year she will finally find the ghost boar responsible. But is there more to the story than she's letting on?

Ghost Boar of the Ringwood

The enormous white boar stamps its feet. Black breath like thick smoke curls from its nose and mouth. With a malign glow in its eyes, the beast charges.

Double strength level 5 troop [BEAST]
Initiative: +9

Gore +10 vs. AC—36 damage. If the ghost boar hit the target on its last turn the attack deals a total of 46 damage on a hit.

C: Ringwood's ebon roots +10 vs. PD (1d3 nearby enemies)—20 negative energy damage
Miss: 10 negative energy damage.

Boatman's blessing: The boar may become ghostly until the end of its turn. While ghostly the boar only does half damage with its *gore* attack and doesn't provoke attacks of opportunity.

Death strike: When the boar drops to 0 hit points or less it may immediately move and make a gore attack. After its attack has been resolved the boar suffers the effects of its current hit points total.

Fear: While engaged with this creature, enemies that have 24 hit points or fewer are dazed (–4 to attack) and do not add the escalation die to their attacks.

AC 16
PD 14   **HP 200**
MD 10

GHOST RIDERS OF MARENA

In the fear-shrouded Principality of Morgau and Doresh, death does not end servitude. In fact, some embrace death as a means to climb the ranks of the principality's powerful army. Second only to the darakhul mercenaries who serve as the army's vanguard, the Order of the Knights Incorporeal is a core of the principality's forces and offers a rare chance for the mortal residents of the realm to serve their dark masters as soldiers instead of as cattle.

SACRIFICED LIFE

The knights begin as living warriors bound to the service of a vampire, necrophagus, or priestess of Marena. Those providing good service for five to ten years may be "raised up" into the ranks of the undead as a foot soldier in the Ghost Knights of Morgau, roughly equivalent to a squire elsewhere. If they continue to perform admirably, and make the transition through ghoul fever or vampiric bite without undue madness or blood frenzy, they can slowly advance through the grades of the Order of the Red Shield.

ONE WITH THE ORDER

Ghost Knights typically ride dappled grey or white warhorses and are equally skilled with lance, mace, and longsword. They often carry a red banner or wear a tabard displaying the insignia of the order (a skull on a red background). Foot soldiers train under the more senior knights, and it's not unusual for several to serve directly under a single Initiate Sister or Honest Brother.

THINGS YOU MIGHT FIND ON A GHOST KNIGHT...

Weapon with a hilt wrapped in red "leather" that is actually part of the knight's mortal form. Weapon made of a black metal that moans and whispers. Bag of grave dirt. Chalice with an insignia of a skull on a red background. Belt containing many small vials of blood in special holsters, each vial carefully labeled with the time of collection and species of "donor". Armor made of bones set in tarnished metal. Purse of 2d20 silver coins, of the type ceremonially buried with the dead in some cultures. Crystal amulet containing a liquid created from distilled nightmares. Crimson badge of rank. Carefully folded certificate of death, emblazoned with the white-skull-on-red. Tattered crimson cloak with a white enamel skull clasp. A map, purporting to show the afterlife and how to navigate it—probably allegorical. Book of poems. Red shield with death-based heraldry on it. Helm styled to look like a skull.

MAGIC ITEMS

Skull Weapon (any melee weapon). The weapon of a ghost knight. *Once per battle:* When you kill a non-mook enemy you may immediately move to engage another enemy without provoking attacks.

Quirk: You take an unnatural interest in blood.

ADVENTURE HOOKS

Bride of Death: The wife of a secret resistance leader in Morgau has joined the ghost knights, hoping to work against the principality's rulers from a position within their ranks. Her husband is unaware of her true plans, and hires the party to kill the undead abomination that he believes his wife to be in the process of becoming. She doesn't want to attack her husband or his tiny but growing resistance movement—but delivering the adventurers to her undead lords might help win their trust.

Ghost Knight of Morgau

The rider stands in the saddle of a dappled horse, his black armor decorated with a dozen red skulls. The wind around him grows still, and the horse seems to shimmer and fade from sight.

Large level 5 troop [UNDEAD]
Initiative: +13

Rearing assault +10 vs. AC—36 damage

Axe of Marena +10 vs. AC—28 negative energy damage
Natural even hit: The ghost knight and its horse (when mounted) become *insubstantial* until the start of its next turn.

[Special trigger] Insubstantial: When an attack targets this creature, the attacker must roll a natural 16+ on the attack roll or it only deals half damage. A hit with holy damage ignores and ends this ability.

C: Death underfoot +10 vs. PD (1d3 nearby or far away enemies)—18 damage as the ghost knight and its steed suddenly seems to be everywhere at once.
Hit or miss: the ghost knight moves as a free action during this attack.

Mounted: The mount and rider are treated as one creature until the rider is dismounted by receiving damage equal to or above a quarter of its maximum hit points (36) in a single attack. When dismounted, the rider and mount are considered separate creatures with their own actions: the rider can use *axe of Marena* and the mount can use *rearing assault* and *death underfoot*. All of their damage is halved, each creature has half of the remaining hit points, and they share defenses and abilities. The rider can remount as a move action.

AC 21
PD 17   **HP 144**
MD 16

Ghostrider Templar

Consecrated to the Red Goddess, the Templar embodies death and havoc.

Large level 7 spoiler [UNDEAD]
Initiative: +15

Shadow blade of Marena +12 vs. PD (one nearby enemy)—30 damage
Natural odd hit: Target becomes weakened (save ends).
Natural even hit: 6 ongoing negative energy damage.
Natural 16+ hit or miss: Include a second target in the attack using the same attack roll.
Natural 18+ hit or miss: Include a third target in the attack using the same attack roll.

Scything death +12 vs. PD (1d3 nearby enemies)—15 damage and the target is blinded (treat as weakened, save ends).

C: Walk of damnation +12 vs. PD (1d3 nearby or far away enemies)—12 ongoing cold damage
Hit or miss: The templar moves as a free action during this attack.

Expanded crit range: The templar crits on a natural 17+.

AC 23
PD 20   **HP 216**
MD 19

GNOMES OF NIEMHEIM

The gnomes of Niemheim were already masters of fey magic and illusion. Now out of terror for the feywitch Baba Yaga they have learned secrets of brimstone and fire-calling from diabolic agents. And they are not afraid to use these powers against potential sacrifices if their woodland charms fail.

CURSED AND BOUND

The winning smiles and easy-going mannerisms of the gnomes of Niemheim hide a dark secret. They are victims of two curses—one of their own making—and must make regular blood sacrifices to preserve their existence.

Roughly 200 years ago, gnomes made a deal with Baba Yaga and it went very, very wrong. They promised her great things: arcane wonders, the blood of kings, the sighs of valkyries, the tears of statues, and the wealth of Mammon. In the past no one had been able to hold the gnomes to the exact letter of their agreements. This time, they promised far too much and delivered far too little to keep Grandmother happy. She swore an oath of vengeance and an oath of fury to destroy the gnomes entirely.

The foolish gnomes were so terrified they made a pact the arch-devils of the Eleven Hells. The gnomes' hellish allies have guarded their forest and shielded the gnomes' twelve villages from the great witch's sight, but the gnomes pay for this service with blood. Whenever possible they sacrifice strangers; but visitors have grown exceedingly rare in the Wormwood. Sacrificing their own to pay the devils' due is no better than succumbing to Baba Yaga's curse, so these once gentle creatures have turned increasingly cold blooded in their attempts to satisfy their infernal protectors.

TRAVELING TRICKSTERS

Those Niemheim gnomes who leave the deep pinewoods of their homeland sometimes make their living as traveling performers and stage magicians. Often encountered on the roads between Holmgard and Courlandia, these prestidigitators offer simple tavern amusement and spin a yarn or two in exchange for food and a room for the night.

Between their card tricks and light shows, the gnomes of Niemheim regale their audiences with tales of their wondrous forest and the hidden gold of the Niemheim king buried beneath the trees. As sure as the sun rises the next morning, some bright-eyed youth or cagey codger has disappeared from the village with a shovel and haversack to claim the gnomes' gold—never to be seen again.

THE WORMWOOD

Niemheim gnomes are defined by their fear of Baba Yaga, and they shelter quietly and modestly among the dark forest boughs of the Wormwood. The forest itself is one of their defining elements; they cut lumber and export it in many forms to Krakova, Morgau, and Vidim, but the trees are more valuable by far for the sense of shelter they give. Their towns and two cities are half above and half below ground, easily overlooked behind fey glamour.

CALL OF THE FLAME

Small creatures native to the Plane of Fire, firegeists sometimes cross over into the material world—or are summoned there by a diabolist. They resemble the smoke from open flame and can easily hide near or within non-magical fire. They take delight in destruction and seek to ignite combustible material so they can feed on the flame and ash. Noted cowards, firegeists always look to strike from ambush and use their natural abilities to hide wherever there is firelight available. Firegeists will flee from any conflict where they don't have the upper hand or if reduced to less than half their hit points.

**THINGS YOU MIGHT FIND
ON A NIEMHEIM GNOME…**

A pouch of coins from around Midgard. Wickedly sharp dagger. Gnomish song book. Tattered hand-bound book of hellish incantations. A map that supposedly shows the way to hidden gold deep in the Wormwood, but actually leads into a trap. Deck of cards. Three little cups and a brightly colored ball. A flute. Gold and silver jewelry stolen from distracted audience members or taken off murdered corpses. Sealed letter to be delivered to a far off town. Belt with pouches. Fancy gnome-sized robes. Sturdy travelling boots. Lock picks sewn into the lining of the left boot.

MAGIC ITEMS

Magic Flute (wondrous item). A golden flute etched with images of capering devils. *Recharge 11+:* Gain +2 to attacks that target MD.

    Recharge 16+: When you play the flute you may make an attack (charisma+level vs MD) against a nearby creature that is not your ally. If you succeed, you cause them to remain nearby you until you stop playing, and you may make another attack against a new non-ally creature. You may continue attempting to enchant creatures until you fail your roll. If you move the enchanted creatures are compelled to follow you for an hour. If an enchanted creature is attacked, the enchantment that compels it to follow you ends. If you are attacked all the enchanted creatures are freed.

    Quirk: Whistle while you plot and scheme.

Juggler's Gloves (gloves/hand). A pair of brightly colored fringed gloves. Gain +4 bonus to juggling and throwing outside of battle.

    Once per battle: When targeted by a ranged weapon attack you may roll a d20. If the roll is higher than the d20 roll of the attack against you then the attack misses you. If the d20 roll is the same as the attack roll you redirect the attack back to the attacker.

    Quirk: You tend to wring your hands and rub them together restlessly. You tell people you're feeling a compulsion to juggle. Actually, you're feeling a compulsion to strangle them.

ADVENTURE HOOKS

Money Is No Object: A badly wounded stranger staggers into town claiming to have been ambushed in the Wormwood by "savage little people with pointy teeth" who were looking for treasure—and offers up the treasure map. A merchant who's stopped for the night immediately offers to finance an expedition, producing enough gold to hire as many baggage handlers, cooks, singers, and non-combatants as the party wishes. Both the stranger and the merchant are disguised gnomes, and the "expedition" is an invitation to be sacrificed.

Niemheim Puck

The gnome smiles, but you see no friendship in the expression. His eyes are too hard, his lips too cruel, and you can detect the faintest whiff of brimstone.

Level 2 caster [HUMANOID]
Initiative: +7

Slicing dagger +7 vs. AC—4 damage
    Natural odd hit: Target is hampered (save ends).
    Natural even hit: +3 psychic damage.

Deft escape: Once per battle the gnome can move without provoking attacks, even if it did not disengage first.

Bend shadows: When the escalation die is even the puck may use a quick action to turn invisible (+5 to all defenses) and it pops free. The puck remains invisible until it next hits with an attack, and the next of its attacks that hits does +7 damage.

AC 18
PD 16   **HP 36**
MD 12

Niemheim Enchanter

Back in the tavern he was a charming entertainer inviting you to pick a card, any card. Now you're on fire and he's trying to carve a hole in your chest.

Level 3 caster [HUMANOID]
Initiative: +10

Sly dagger +8 vs. AC—10 damage
    Natural 16+ hit or miss: The target becomes vulnerable to the enchanter's attacks until the end of the enchanter's next turn.

R: Arcane bolt +8 vs. PD—10 damage
    Natural 16+ hit or miss: The target becomes vulnerable to the enchanter's attacks until the end of the enchanter's next turn.

C: Call flame—A curtain of fire appears between the gnome and its foes. Anyone currently engaged with the gnome takes 10 fire damage and pops free. Until the start of the gnome's next turn ranged attacks against the gnome take a -4 to hit, and anyone who engages the gnome in melee takes 10 fire damage.

Burning allies: When staggered, as a quick action the gnome summons 2d12 firegeists who fight on its behalf. The firegeists remain in the battle until they die or the enchanter has 0 hit points or less.

Leyline leap: Once per battle when the gnome is hit by a melee attack, the gnome ignores the attack and teleports anywhere nearby that it can see.

AC 17
PD 13   **HP 45**
MD 16

Firegeist

Summoned forth to do the bidding of another, it dances like smoke and burns like fire.

Level 1 mook [ABERRATION]
Initiative: +3
Vulnerable: cold

Fire lash +6 vs. AC—4 ongoing fire damage

Flickering flame: When the firegeist is missed by a melee attack it pops free and the enemy that missed it takes 4 fire damage.

Combustion: Any enemy that ends its turn engaged with the firegeist takes 4 ongoing fire damage.

Resist fire 16+: When a fire attack targets this creature, the attacker must roll a natural 16+ on the attack roll or it only deals half damage.

AC 16
PD 12   **HP 7 (mook)**
MD 12

Mook: Kill one firegeist mook for every 7 damage you deal to the mob.

Niemheim Choirmaster

There is a special place reserved in the afterlife for choirmasters. A very WARM place...

Level 3 caster [HUMANOID]
Initiative: +9

Cunning dagger +8 vs. AC—10 damage

R: Hellish pitch +8 vs. PD—8 thunder damage and the target is vulnerable to all attacks until the start of its next turn
  Natural 18+ hit or miss: Target pops free.

R: Soul capture +8 vs. MD (one nearby or far away staggered enemy)—5 fire damage and 5 ongoing negative energy damage
  First failed save: Ongoing damage increases by 5 and the target is stuck (save ends both).
  Second failed save: The target disappears from this plane for 5 full rounds or until the choirmaster is next hit, whichever comes first. While gone the target can use the *fight in spirit* rules to aid its companions but can take no other actions.

AC 18
PD 13   **HP 45**
MD 17

GOBLIN SHARK

Incredibly ugly and unnerving, these gilled goblins are somewhat larger and leaner than their terrestrial cousins and possess a protruding shelf of a nose overhanging an incredibly wide mouth packed with multiple rows of sharp, triangular teeth. Their large noses are hard, thick protuberances that grant them a keen sense of smell. Goblin sharks raise their young in specially evolved incubation pouches. Wily goblin sharks distend their massive jaws to swallow and hide small objects within these pouches. Able to take the shape of equally ugly shark-like creatures, packs of goblin sharks patrol shallow coral reefs in search of food while terrorizing fishermen and merchant ships.

Entire tribes of goblin sharks dwell in caves carved from dead reefs or within the sunken ruins of forgotten empires, and areas that host such a tribe are typically filthy and polluted. Like their land-bound cousins, goblin sharks are superstitious and make use of all manner of flotsam to create primitive weapons, clothes, and tools. The less scrupulous among dockside communities often form partnerships with rogue packs of goblin sharks, taking advantage of their ability to consume and regurgitate small items to bypass port fees and taxes and bring in items they do not wish to declare to the authorities.

THINGS YOU MIGHT FIND ON A GOBLIN SHARK...

A shark-tooth edged sword. Shark-tooth necklace. Shark-skin loincloth. Damp hood and cloak. Driftwood club. Collection of rings (some with fingers still in them) inside their smuggling pouch. Shell-shard dagger. Auger (for making holes in the bottom of ships). Seaweed-woven clothing. Sea-water stiffened leather wrappings. Over-large shirt with old stains, worn with a rope belt as a tunic. Starfish in brine, in a small bottle. Fishing hook earrings. Lantern on a stick (used for luring ships onto a reef). Gold earrings. Small carved ivory fish-hook necklace. Map of a port.

Goblin Shark

A four-foot-tall goblin emerges from the waves and crawls along the shore, shedding its shark-like form and grinning with an impossibly wide mouth filled with rows of sharp teeth.

Level 2 troop [HUMANOID]
Initiative: +9

Bite +10 vs. AC—4 ongoing damage
Miss: 4 damage
[Special] See *change shape* for possible bonuses to hit and damage.

Shortsword +10 vs. AC—7 damage
[Special] Must be in goblin form.

Aquatic: The goblin shark can breathe under water just as well as it breathes air, and is an expert swimmer. It can detect blood in water up to a mile away, and locate an enemy even in pitch darkness or murky water.

Smuggler's pouch: As a quick action the goblin shark swallows (or disgorges) a small object from its incubation pouch. Objects in the pouch cannot be targeted by enemies.

Change Shape: The goblin shark may alter its physical form to appear as a small shark or goblin. Doing so is a free action if it is leaving or entering water; otherwise it is a quick action. When in an aquatic environment in shark form, it gains +2 to hit and damage with *bite* attacks when fighting a non-aquatic foe.

AC 15
PD 13   **HP 36**
MD 9

Goblin Shark Shaman

Deep waters conceal many secrets...

Level 2 caster [HUMANOID]
Initiative: +9

Bite +10 vs. AC—4 ongoing damage
Miss: 4 damage
[Special] See *change shape* for possible bonuses to hit and damage.

Coral rod +10 vs. AC—7 damage
[Special] Must be in goblin form.

R: Stinging tendrils +10 vs. PD—4 lightning damage and 4 ongoing poison damage
Miss: Can use *ink cloud* as a quick action

R: Ink cloud +10 vs. PD (1d3 nearby or far away enemies in a group)—target is dazed (save ends).

Aquatic: The goblin shark can breathe under water just as well as it breathes air, and is an expert swimmer. It can detect blood in water up to a mile away, and locate an enemy even in pitch darkness or murky water.

Smuggler's pouch: As a quick action the goblin shark swallows (or disgorges) a small object from its incubation pouch. Objects in the pouch cannot be targeted by enemies.

Change Shape: The goblin shark may alter its physical form to appear as a small shark or goblin. Doing so is a free action if it is leaving or entering water; otherwise it is a quick action. When in an aquatic environment in shark form, it gains +2 to hit and damage with *bite* attacks when fighting a non-aquatic foe.

AC 15
PD 13   **HP 36**
MD 9

GOBLINS OF THE WASTED WEST

The Old Ones did it. They changed the buggers. It wasn't the heat, or lack of food, or just not being civilized. These goblins live in the shadow of another world and can't be compared to anything natural in all of Midgard. No one creature better represents the corruption and variety of the dangers in the Wasted West than the goblin. Nowhere else in Midgard will you find a race so different from tribe to tribe.

The goblins below are but a small selection of the unique goblin cultures found throughout this unforgiving land...

GHOST GOBLIN TRIBE

The Ghost Goblins have strong ties to their dead in more than just a spiritual sense. When their warriors die, tribal necromancers create unliving soldiers to fill the ranks. So devoted are they to this practice that the undead obey all members of the tribe instinctively, even those with no talent for spells.

Some warriors among the Ghost Goblins hold the undead in higher esteem than the living. They strive to honor the zombies through their actions, and through prayers to strange gods. Soon a ghost goblin horror is born, too intelligent to be considered a zombie but too unnatural to be called a living creature.

As its flesh slowly begins to rot away, a horror begins to develop a talent for tugging at the souls of others. The horror exists halfway between life and death, suffering vulnerabilities of both the living and unliving. This place between worlds grants it power, however. The ghost goblin horror can implant the suggestion of death in an enemy's mind, paralyzing its body with the rigor of the dead before attacking relentlessly. The ghost goblin horror does not fear death and will retreat from battle only if ordered by a necromancer or priest.

DUST DIGGER TRIBE

The Dust Diggers scour the waste in search of long abandoned artifacts. These strange goblins seem supernaturally talented in getting vril technology working again. Most members have an odd vril trinket in their arsenal. Some of them have even modified their bodies, seeming more construct than flesh.

The dust digger watchmen are charged with protecting the excavations of the tribe. They take up a position that grants cover and makes them difficult to see, whenever possible, but do not sacrifice proximity to the excavation site. When enemies come too near, the watchman opens fire and shouts for reinforcements. Watchmen typically fight alongside other warriors, and support mobile skirmishers well. Dust Diggers are also found with strange constructs and war machines excavated from vril ruins.

BONEWRAITH TRIBE

The cannibalistic bonewraith tribe are speakers with spirits, and some say with the Old Ones themselves. Ceremonial leaders among the bonewraith tribe, the spirit callers are masters of ritual and can commune with large numbers of spirits. Their bone weapons and tools are carved with beautiful—if disturbing—images, and their hide armor bears the grisly, weathered faces of former enemies.

AARON MILLER

Spirit callers generally partake of goblin flesh more than other tribesmen. They can be recognized by their twitching hands and over-dilated pupils. In combat they can connect to an enemy's soul and then use this connection to force their target's limbs to move against the victim's will.

The Bonewraith tribe generally doesn't work with non-goblins, but they may make temporary alliances and do on occasion tame beasts as mounts or combatants.

THINGS YOU MIGHT FIND ON A GHOST GOBLIN HORROR...

Tiny bone disks carved with goblin prayers. Metal helm, exhortations to strange gods scratched into it. Maggots fat from the flesh of the decaying goblin. Mismatched pieces of armor, scavenged or taken from the bodies of slain enemies.

THINGS YOU MIGHT FIND ON A DUST DIGGER TRIBE GOBLIN...

Large bone knife. Chest containing broken artifacts. Goggles. Pliers. Tarnished coins with holes drilled into them, and star-charts scratched into their faces. Map of the wastes. Warm rock which glows slightly in the dark. Tea pot. Necklace of steel teeth. Dowsing rod. String of sand-glass beads. Jar containing a twisting bit of frozen time—if unfrozen over a fire it reveals the last words of a dying wizard. A chest containing 49 smaller chests, one inside the other, until the final chest which contains a tiny cloth doll.

THINGS YOU MIGHT FIND ON A BONEWRAITH GOBLIN...

Armor made from the faces of victims. Bone sword, made out of the bones of victims. Pouch, made out of the skin of victims. Trousers, made out of the flesh of victims. Vile totem made out of soulstuff and bones.

MAGIC ITEMS

Vril Power Bow (bow). A priceless artifact from a lost time, but sadly not as reliable as it was when it was new. At the start of each of your turns, roll a d8. If you roll over the escalation die value, on a successful hit with this weapon add the die result to your damage and the target briefly glows. If you roll under the escalation die, you take the die result in damage and you briefly glow. Rolling equal to the escalation die applies no damage from the roll, but you can make another attack with the bow on this turn as a quick action.

Quirk: Dream of lost ages, seek to restore that which was lost.

Goblin Totem (holy or unholy symbol). The artifact is unmistakably goblin in design, but started life as a holy symbol for a different god. Gain +1 to hit for every goblin ally in the battle, including yourself if you are a goblin, to a maximum of +6.

Recharge 16+ (**Ghost Goblin tribal totem**): On a successful hit with a single-target melee attack, the target is seized with rigor mortis (stuck, save ends).

Recharge 16+ (**Bonewraith tribal totem**): On a successful hit with a single-target melee attack against a foe with half your total hit points or fewer, the target is terrified by a vision of goblin ancestral spirits (fear, save ends).

Recharge 16+ (**Dust Digger tribal totem**): On a successful hit with a single-target ranged attack, the target is dazed by powerful vril energy (save ends).

Quirk: Sing traditional goblin songs such as "Three Dirty Goblins", "The Goblin's Eyes" and "Goblin's Lament". If you sing the songs for long enough they may drift into unholy hymns to the Old Ones without you noticing.

ADVENTURE HOOKS

The Goblin Market: A shiver of goblin sharks have come to town, far from their home, to meet and trade with representatives of the bonewraith tribe. The situation is potentially explosive—especially as the items the bonewraiths are trading belong to the ghost goblins, and the shark goblin's items were stolen from dust diggers.

Ghost Goblin Horror

The ghost goblin horror fights alongside other living and undead tribe members. Sometimes the tribe will take in undead discovered in travels and raids. These creatures were often not goblins in life, so there is no end to the variety of undead they might command.

Level 2 troop [UNDEAD]
Initiative: +5
Vulnerable: holy

Short sword +6 vs. AC—5 damage
  Natural even hit or miss: The goblin may use *curse of rigor* as a quick action.

   R: Curse of rigor +6 vs. MD—5 damage and the target is stuck (save ends).

   Ghost life: When the ghost goblin horror is reduced to 0 hit points it makes a save. If it succeeds it gains 5 hit points and regenerates 5 hit points per turn until the end of the battle or it is next reduced to 0 hit points.

   Fear aura: Enemies engaged with the goblin and who have 12 hit points or less are dazed and can't use the escalation die.

   AC 17
   PD 11 **HP 27**
   MD 15

Dust Digger Watchman

Dust digger watchmen guard major excavation sites against looters. Surprisingly disciplined, these goblins know the power of the artifacts they seek. They have mastered the strange vril bows whose bolts are charged with the power of the sun. When they open fire, reinforcements are never far behind.

Level 2 archer [HUMANOID]
Initiative: +8

War pick +7 vs. AC—7 damage

R: Vril powerbow +7 vs. AC—7 holy damage
 Natural 16+ hit: Target glows and is vulnerable to all
   attacks until the end of its next turn.

AC 18
PD 16   **HP 36**
MD 12

Bonewraith Spirit Caller

The Bonewraith goblins are known for eating both their enemies and the weak and fallen of their own tribe. They fashion the resulting bones into weapons, totems, and armor, to imbue themselves with the power of the fallen. Most who encounter these fearsome creatures flee rather than find out the truth of these claims.

Level 2 caster [HUMANOID]
Initiative: +6

Bone sword +7 vs. AC—7 damage

R: Soul grasp +7 vs. MD—7 damage and the target pops free

R: Summon ancestors +7 vs. PD—7 damage
 Natural 18+ hit or miss: Causes fear in 1d3 nearby enemies
   (save ends).

[Triggered action] Spirit guardian: When the spirit caller becomes
   staggered it gains +2 to all its defenses until it is next hit.

AC 18
PD 16   **HP 36**
MD 12

R. HERSHEY - 11

Golems

Golems are creatures made of durable materials and given life through complex and ancient rituals. Some say that the giants made the first golems in imitation of their primordial creators. Others look no further than humanity's ability and desire to twist the ley lines to its own purpose. Whatever the origin, the process is imperfect, creating only near mindless creatures incapable of true moral choices.

MONSTER, NOT MAN

The lengthy process of creating a golem begins with crafting the body, a painstakingly precise and often very expensive endeavor. Each part must be functional and strong enough to survive the rituals and contain the animating power, thus often requiring a master's skill to construct.

Golems are almost unthinking creatures who obey their master's orders precisely and with little capacity for improvisation should the situation change. While this makes them excellent guardians, willing to wait centuries until their orders trigger, it also makes them very dangerous. Poorly worded orders often lead to misinterpretations, and only destruction will stop a golem from completing what it thinks it must do, whatever its master's true intent. Careless phrasing of orders had brought down many otherwise intelligent and clever people.

POWERED
FROM ANOTHER WORLD

Unlike mechanical constructs, golems are not composed of springs and gears and mechanisms. Instead, some spark of outside energy animates each golem. This most commonly comes from a link, created during the final ritual, to one of the elemental planes, allowing the essence of living earth, lightning, air, or fire to animate the construct. The rituals vary, however. Some may channel the power of divinity, while others link to much darker powers.

MAGIC ITEMS

Greathammer (hammer, 2-handed heavy). An oversize two-handed hammer, lighter than it looks but difficult to stop once it is moving. Giant axes and swords also exist. *Recharge 16+:* You may reroll any damage result that is below the escalation die value, and use the second result.
Quirk: Might makes right.

Warfist (1-handed heavy melee weapon). This huge magical glove is made from the hand of a golem. It is useless for grasping things, but it can crush and make magically enhanced punches. On a successful attack, deal miss damage to every additional foe with whom you're engaged.
Quirk: Smash objects when angry. Get angry when not smashing objects.

ADVENTURE HOOKS

The Fallen Idol: A group of goblins have taken to worshiping a damaged steam golem as a god. The golem rampages mindlessly, and the goblins follow in white robes blessing it from a safe distance. The cult supports itself by picking through the rubble for shiny trinkets.

Death Among the Sands: A party of wealthy nobles have set up a large dig at a recently rediscovered lost desert city, despite the warnings of those who know better. Their activities have awoken several glass golems who visit the camp at night to enact grisly revenge.

Eye Golem

The eye golem is a giant, powerful creature that almost glows in dim light. It stands at least ten feet tall, and its skin is covered with real eyes as well as tattoos of arcane sigils that resemble eyes. The eye golem rarely kills its opponents but rather steals their eyes once they hover on the verge of death. The victims become permanently blind but tormented by visions of the eye golem flashing through their memory. Many go mad. Others instead serve the golem, becoming devoted to the one who still holds sight.

When killed, all of an eye golem's eyes open at once. It releases a scream heard for miles and a burst of light that blots out everything around. When the light and noise stop, hundreds of perfectly preserved eyeballs remain on the ground all around. The eyes are still warm and fresh, without scars or damage.

Careful examination of the eye golem's eyes (DC 24 Wisdom check) reveals that many of them have a thin beam of arcane energy connecting them to their owners. Those who claim the central eye once the monster is slain can use it to restore stolen eyes to past victims or as a focus for divination rituals.

Eye Golem

A muscular giant stands alert, its well-proportioned body and smooth, marble-white skin covered with eye-like sigils. One of the sigils opens for a moment, and a beam like sunlight shines forth to pierce the night.

Large level 8 spoiler [CONSTRUCT]
Initiative: +16

Withering hand +10 vs. AC (+13 vs AC if the target is staggered)—66 damage
Natural 16+ hit: Target is blinded (treat as weakened), takes 10 ongoing damage and takes a -2 to hit any foe except the eye golem (save ends all).

C: Gaze of ancient light +13 vs. PD (1d3 nearby enemies)— Target is weakened and stuck (save ends both).
First failed save: Target takes 20 holy damage.
Second failed save: Target takes 30 ongoing holy damage and the *ancient light* blazes from the target's body, dealing 5 holy damage to all of the target's nearby allies at the start of the target's turn (save by the target ends).
Limited use: The eye golem must be staggered to use this attack.

C: Primal voice of doom +13 vs. MD (1d3 nearby or far away enemies)—66 damage and target is weakened (save ends).
Limited use: The eye golem must be staggered to use this attack.

Piercing sight: The eye golem never takes penalties to ranged attack rolls.

Shoot into the sunbeam: The eye golem gains a +2 bonus to defenses against all ranged attacks and a +2 bonus to defenses against opportunity attacks.

Threatening reach: The eye golem can make opportunity attacks against nearby foes with whom it's not engaged.

AC 24
PD 22   **HP 288**
MD 18

Glass Golem

These massive creatures seem carved from obsidian, with sharp angles and an unnaturally dark sheen, though the glass that makes them up is fantastically sturdy. Almost always humanoid, these sand-blown monstrosities are a bane to both melee warriors and spell-slingers.

GIANT ORIGINS

Supposedly the giants of the legendary floating city of Kadralhu crafted the first glass golems. With Kadralhu's ruins recently uncovered in the Ishmai desert, scholars can now study the remains of some of the earliest known glass golems.

The sand giants of Ishmai believe that the fact that these golems were made from glass, and therefore sand, instead of a more traditional material presents a strong link to their own origins. Many parts of Kadralhu remain unexplored and could hold more clues to these golems' origins, and to the giants' distant past as well.

SHADOW SOULS

Glass golems almost always appear black, no matter the original color of the glass. Though very rare, however, brightly colored glass golems do exist. Some speculate that the animating ritual draws energy from the Plane of Shadow and clouds the glass while providing the spark of life. The glass is too dark to be reflective, though some bards tell of a young man mesmerized while examining the flat surface of a golem and later reporting a vision of a gaunt man, unlike himself, staring back at him.

Glass Golem

The two statues stir, their black glass limbs clinking and grinding as they step from the wall niches. They raise their immense glass hands aggressively and shout unintelligible words in deep, resonant voices.

Large level 8 troop [CONSTRUCT]
Initiative: +16

Obsidian fist +13 vs. AC—50 damage
Miss: 25 damage.
Natural 16+ hit: The golem can make another *obsidian fist* attack as a free action.

Ancient glass: Once per round when the golem is hit by an attack that does typed damage (acid, cold, fire, etc) it triggers a *magical refraction* attack.

[Special trigger] **C: Magical refraction +13 vs. PD (1d6 nearby enemies)**—46 damage of the same type as the triggering attack.

Golem rampage: Once per round as a quick action the golem moves and makes 1d3 *obsidian fist* attacks during its movement.

Limited use: The golem starts each battle with only one use of *golem rampage*. Every round the escalation die is odd, it gains another use of the ability.

Splintering glass: When the golem takes damage, all enemies engaged with it take 15 damage.

Bloody shards: When the golem is staggered, any creature hit by one of its attacks takes 25 ongoing damage.

AC 24
PD 22   **HP 288**
MD 18

STEAM GOLEM

Built around a central boiler, with clockwork gearing and hydraulic presses powering its legs and arms, a steam golem stands eight feet tall and measures four feet wide at the shoulders. Its eyes typically glow orange or red from its internal fires. It has four to six vents for releasing steam as needed. A steam golem's whistles are usually mounted over the shoulders, in the "ear" location, or sometimes at the elbows. If kept active for many hours, its boiler glows cherry red with heat.

DESIGNED FOR COMBAT

Two large arm blades constitute a steam golem's standard armament. The steam golem normally attacks by moving its arms together to create a massive great axe and strikes with a surprising grace. The creature is smart enough to operate independently and knows that its strength lies in melee. It always attempts to use its superior speed to close quickly. Once in the thick of battle, it uses its shrieking whistle to disrupt ranged attackers and vents steam if its foes bunch together.

WILD CORE

The key to the steam golem's great power resides in its central boiler design. The outer shell of the creature is built of the finest metal available and magically treated. It acts not only as armor but also as a cage. Unlike other golems, the final step in the animation process summons and traps a powerful elemental within the boiler prison. Skilled mages call forth fire elementals for this process, adding water as needed to produce the proper steam. The most skilled arcanists call forth much rarer steam elementals and thus avoid the need for further maintenance.

Steam Golem

With wicked axe-blades inset along its arms, bronze runes inlaid on its armored torso, and a cast-iron belly glowing red with fiery heat, this heavy construct looks to be a deadly machine.

Large level 11 wrecker [CONSTRUCT]
Initiative: +22

Arm blade +16 vs. AC—90 damage
  Miss: 30 damage.

Great axe +16 vs. AC—120 damage

Steam vent: The first time the golem becomes staggered in a battle it immediately makes a *steam vent* attack.
[Special Trigger] **Steam vent +16 vs. AC (1d3 nearby enemies)**—90 fire damage
Natural 16+ hit: Target is dazed (save ends).

  Steam leak: While the golem is staggered any enemy who starts its turn engaged with the golem immediately takes 45 fire damage.

  Whistle: Once per round when the steam golem is hit by a ranged attack it makes a *thunder whistle* attack.
  [Special trigger] **C: Thunder whistle +16 vs. PD (the one nearby or far away enemy who hit the steam golem)**—90 thunder damage
  Natural 16+ hit: Target is weakened (save ends) and the triggering attack does half damage.

AC 27
PD 25   **HP 576**
MD 21

HORAKH

Even battle-hardened dungeoneers quiver at the mention of the horakh. These bloodthirsty insects travel in small packs and make lightning-fast attacks against the weak and vulnerable. Horakh do not always immediately consume their prey. They occasionally use the maimed as bait to capture other creatures. Some say the horakh will even herd blind victims like sheep back to their hidden colony deep in the bowels of the earth to a fate unknown.

EATERS OF EYES

Horakh have powerful rear legs that allow them to make bounding leaps. Sharp hooks on each powerful claw make it easy for them to climb any surface and latch on to prey. The scooped mandibles dominating their heads shoot forward like pistons to shear meat from bone. Their black, chitinous thoraxes are topped by a translucent digestive sac containing the half-dissolved eyeballs from a variety of creatures.

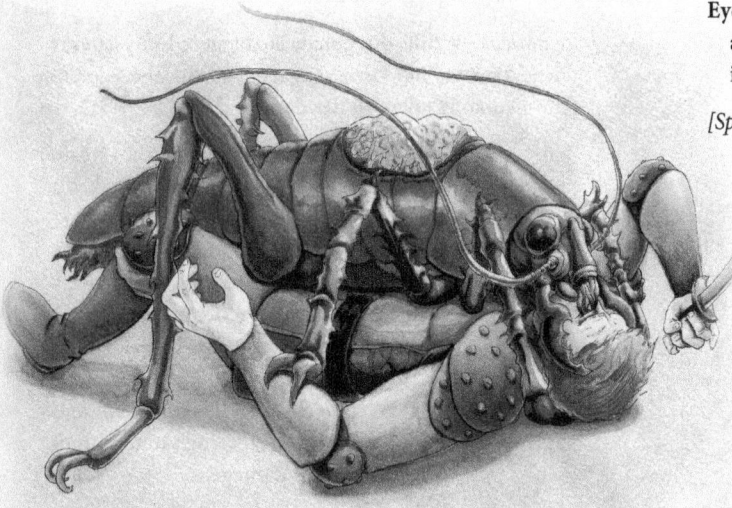

POUNCE FROM HIDING

Horakh silently skulk at the edges of larger groups of monsters, waiting to pick off the weak and wounded. Eyeless beasts, such as grimlocks, destrachan, and gricks have nothing to fear from horakh and often tolerate losing some spoils of battle to them for the sake of mutual protection. When attacking, horakh leap from hiding with a deafening screech.

Generally, horakh first attempt to grab and slash victims and once they are on a victim try to scoop out the victim's eyeballs. Horakh are highly mobile. If threatened, they leap back into the shadows to attack again from a more advantageous position. They rarely fight to the death and flee if the assault goes poorly. Horakh have been known to harry travelers over the course of many days, looking for a weakness in their defenses.

MAGIC ITEMS

Horakh Eyes (wondrous item). These iridescent orbs are made of polished horakh chitin, and orbit their owner's head. Roll two d20s for any skill rolls involving vision. Also, on a successful hit with any ranged attack you can add the value of the escalation die to the damage.

Quirk: Eyes are precious. Collect them.

Horakh

In the deepest recesses of dungeons and caverns, hideous creatures struggle for survival. Life is short and brutal. Only the most vicious live to breed and fight another day. Among the most feared subterranean denizens is the horakh, an insectoid killing machine with a penchant for consuming the eyes of its victim. The giant insect's antennae twitch and its vicious mandibles clack. You see a semi-transparent sac on its back pulse as the creature's ovipositor shifts forward and it crouches to leap.

Level 5 spoiler [BEAST]
Initiative: +17

Claw slash +10 vs. AC—10 damage
Natural odd hit: Target is grabbed.
Natural even hit: The horakh makes a second *claw slash* attack as a quick action.
Miss: The horakh pops free and moves as a quick action.

Eye scoop attack +10 vs. PD (one grabbed enemy)—10 damage and the target is dazed (save ends). On a critical hit the target is blinded (treat as weakened) until the end of the encounter.

[Special trigger]: Ovipositor: When the horakh reduces a grabbed creature to 0 hit points it makes an eye scoop attack against the target as a coup de grace. If successful the horakh scoops out one of its target's eyes (use the lasting wound rule in chapter 5 of the 13th Age core rulebook.) It also jams its ovipositor deep into the target's eye socket and inserts a pebble-sized egg. Instead of dying from these wounds the target is stabilized and contracts horakh incubation disease.

Horakh Incubation
Incubation starts at stage 1. At each full heal-up the target makes a DC 20 constitution check. A success moves the disease down one stage, a failure moves it up one stage.
Stage 0: The target recovers from the disease.
Stage 1: While affected by stage 1, the target takes a -2 penalty to MD.
Stage 2: While affected by stage 2, the target suffers from constant, debilitating migraines. Target cannot make attacks against far away creatures, and takes a -2 penalty to all defenses.
Stage 3: While affected by stage 3, the target must make an easy save twice a day. If they fail both saves a horakh explodes from their head, and they die.

Leap and skitter: The horakh can leap from far away to engage an enemy with a single move action. The creature can move on walls and ceilings as easily as it does on the ground.

Nastier Special
Deafening Screech: Until the start of the horakh's next turn, all nearby enemies take a -4 to spell attack rolls *Limited use:* Once per battle.

AC 21
PD 15   **HP 72**
MD 19

ICE MAIDEN

Found in the freezing Northlands of Midgard, ice maidens are the daughters of powerful creatures. Some descend from Boreas, God of the North Wind, or the Snow Queen of Frozen Reach, but they are occasionally born to frost giants and thursir, or result from tearful pleas by pregnant women lost in the snows and desperate to save their unborn child.

YEARNING FOR LOVE

Most ice maidens live solitary lives, save for a thrall or two. They are lonely creatures, desperate for love but condemned to know it only through their magical kisses which freeze their paramour's heart. It is said that if genuine love ever fills an ice maiden's heart, she will literally melt into nothingness. Occasionally, three ice maidens will band together in a coven - more to ease loneliness than for power (ice maidens working together can control more thralls).

THINGS YOU MIGHT FIND ON AN ICE MAIDEN...

Clothing made of furs and silks. Diamond diadem. Lots of other items that look like they are made of glass or diamond but melt as soon as they leave the possession of the ice maiden.

MAGIC ITEMS

Ice Maiden's Cloak (cloak). A warm fur cloak—a little too warm. You are immune to non-magical cold. Also, whenever you would take cold damage you subtract your level from the damage total (potentially reducing it to 0). Whenever you take fire damage, add your level to the damage taken.
Quirk: It's never cold enough for you.

ADVENTURE HOOKS

Desire of the Ice Maiden: An ice maiden has become tired of being fought over by rival ice giants, and yearns to get away from it all. The adventurers seem to enjoy a life of such glorious freedom—why not join them? She starts to follow after the party, proving a valuable companion in battle. Unfortunately, the ice giants now have a common enemy to vent their jealous rage on.

Snow-Crossed Lovers: A noted swordsman has returned to his home in the south with a new wife, a stunning pale beauty. But her mother the Snow Queen isn't happy about the union, and an unnatural winter descends—bringing strange monsters from the Northlands with it.

Ice Maiden

This alluring beauty has skin and hair as white as snow, and eyes blue as glacial ice.

Level 5 caster [HUMANOID]
Initiative: +14
Vulnerable: fire

Frost dagger +10 vs. AC—36 cold damage

Kiss of the frozen heart +10 vs. MD—Target becomes confused and does not take damage from cold-based attacks. Both conditions end if the target makes a hard save, the ice maiden is reduced to 0 hit points or less, or the target is kissed by a loved one. If the target is still affected by the *kiss of the frozen heart* at the end of the battle, the effect lasts until the ice maiden fails to kiss the target during a 24-hour period, or until the ice maiden is reduced to 0 hit points or less.
Limited use: Once per battle, but if it misses its use is not expended.

C: Freezing north winds +10 vs. PD (one nearby enemy)—20 cold damage

R: Snowblind burst +10 vs. PD (1d3 nearby or far away enemies in a group)—36 cold damage and the target is blinded (treat as weakened.)
Miss: 18 cold damage.
Limited use: This ability can only be used when the escalation die is odd.

Flurry Form: As a quick action the ice maiden disperses into a swirling snow cloud. While in flurry form, the ice maiden can be targeted only by fire attacks, and can use only her *freezing north winds* attack. She can fly, squeeze through openings as though she were a flurry of snow, and does not provoke attacks of opportunity. The ice maiden can resume her normal form as a quick action. She must resume her humanoid form after taking damage from a fire attack, or after using *freezing north winds*.

Snow invisibility: If the ice maiden is in a snowy environment, she may turn invisible as a move action (+5 to all defenses). This effect ends when she makes an attack.

Ice eyes: Ice maidens can see perfectly in snowy conditions, including driving blizzards.

Chilling presence: An enemy that starts its turn engaged with the ice maiden becomes vulnerable to cold until the end of their next turn.

AC 20
PD 19   **HP 144**
MD 17

IMPERIAL GHAST CENTURION

Many ghouls are condemned from their creation to scrabble after scraps, while other rise to be masters of the underworld. Only the highly variable course of the disease that creates ghouls—best known as ghoul fever or "the curtain" among ghouls—separates these two groups. The worst-off become ordinary ghouls or ghasts. They remember essentially nothing of their former lives, and their minds sink to a lower state of hunger, rage, and more hunger. The fortunate ones retain some of their memories and skills to become imperial ghasts and ghouls, the Imperium's middle class.

ELITE COMMANDERS

Ghast centurions lead the empire's ghouls and ghast shock troops. They charge into battle on beetle-back and understand both the chain of command and military strategy. Ghast centurions work hard to improve their status and most resent the darakhul, who sit above them in ghoul society.

DESPERATE FOR MORE POWER

Many believe that the hunger cults or the necrophagi know the secret of transforming imperial ghasts and ghouls into darakhul. These rumors give the ghast centurions hope of advancement, and their power over lesser ghouls and slaves gives them a tantalizing taste of tyranny. Ambitious, they constantly strive to prove themselves as leaders, warriors, or spies. Although they often enter battle armed with greataxes and longspears, many quickly resort to their claws and teeth due to their insatiable hunger and blood lust.

THINGS YOU MIGHT FIND ON AN IMPERIAL GHAST CENTURION...

Black leather under-robes, with chains of rank. Skull and blackened plate armor. Greataxe. Longspear. Dagger bearing the Imperial crest. Pouch containing written orders, maps, and notebooks. Shield with the three-skulls emblem of their masters.

Imperial Ghast Centurion

The foul creature wears black plate mail, carries a shield marked with crests of the Ghoul Imperium, and brandishes an enormous spear. "Hold!" it calls. "Stand fast in the name of the Empire!"

Double strength level 5 troop [UNDEAD]
Initiative: +13

Steel-shod claws +10 vs. AC—21 damage
Natural odd hit: 10 ongoing negative energy damage.
Natural even hit: Target is hampered (save ends).

C: Longspear +10 vs. AC (one nearby enemy)—24 damage
Miss: 12 damage.
Critical hit: Target is hampered (save ends).
[special] The ghast crits with this attack on a natural 18+. Every time the ghast crits with this attack, its crit range expands by 1.

R: Crossbow +10 vs. AC—18 damage
Natural even hit: Make another *crossbow* attack as a quick action.

Imperial conscription: When an enemy that the ghast kills dies, the ghast may choose to have it reanimate as a new ghast centurion within 1d4 hours. The newly risen ghast is under the control of the original ghast. Only humanoid, non-construct, non-undead creatures rise. Usually a ghast can use this power twice only, ever. Magical rituals might prevent the slain enemy rising as a ghast.

Glory to the emperor: When the ghast first becomes staggered (reduced to 72 hit points or less) it may immediately make an attack as a free action against any single foe within range, and it regains 20 hit points.

Fear aura: Enemies engaged with the ghast and who have 24 hit points or less are dazed and can't use the escalation die.

AC 20
PD 19   **HP 144**
MD 17

IRONCRAG DWARVES

The peaks of the Ironcrags rank among the most unforgiving lands in Midgard. Nestled deep within these mountains, the stalwart dwarves and other humanoids of the Ironcrag Cantons live freely and proudly in service to no feudal lords. Any who look back too fondly on the days of the dwarven monarchy soon find another place to live. In fact, many monarchist dwarves have found homes in the northern areas of the Seven Cities.

THINGS YOU MIGHT FIND ON A DWARF…

Sturdy boots. Leather trousers. Big sturdy mug. Leather kilt and a sporran (sporran contains a sharp bone-handled knife and a tiny brass key). A small pouch containing 10d10 gp in gems. A large heavy pouch containing 100+d20 sp and 3d20 cp. A fold of leather containing five gold coins, each with the name of a dwarf scratched into it. Large, ornate iron key. Lock of braided hair worn in a neck pouch, together with a dwarven love poem. Broken lock. Dwarven pocket tool containing many fold out blades and other useful devices. Map, half drawn. Ledger, engineering notebook or recipe book, and graphite stub. Ten candles of different colors. Codpiece shaped like a snarling badger head. Frying pan with a slight head-shaped dent. Wrapped in a clean cloth: a cheese and mushroom pastry, a baked potato, and a small clay bottle of mead. Lots of leather belts, each with several pouches containing different kinds of stones and the exterior of each pouch has a different rune on it. Lodestone. Plumb line. Drinking horn.

MAGIC ITEMS

Ironcrag Shield (shield). The shield bears many anvil designs around the edge, and rings loudly when struck with a hammer. *Recharge 6+:* When fighting with a hammer, reroll any damage dice that come up 1s until they are no longer 1s (2s at Champion tier, 3s at epic tier).

   Quirk: Sing the dwarven battle songs of the Ironcrags. If you don't know any, you make them up.

Ancestral Weapon (any hammer or axe). This weapon has been handed down from generation to generation.

   Once per battle: Before you roll your attack you may lower the bonus you add to your attack roll, and add that amount to your damage on a hit. If you miss the power is not expended and you gain +2 to your next attack roll.

   Quirk: You are obsessed with what your ancestors would think of your actions, and strive to be worthy of them.

ADVENTURE HOOKS

The Cup of the Sun: A legendary golden drinking goblet, long thought to be pure myth, has turned up for auction. Dwarves of all stripes flock to see it. After several attempted thefts the party is hired to safeguard the goblet until it is sold. Dwarves have turned up dead, there are fights in the street, and the auction itself promises to be a riot. But is the goblet authentic?

Dwarf Berserker

Dwarves prosper in the Northlands as well, though in a very different sort of way. The northern dwarves keep the old ways and the old gods—smiths and warriors, farmers and traders, these stout and strong individuals can reputedly down a barrel of ale. They often fight giants or werewolves and wargs in the north, but sometimes these dwarves take to the sea in their longships and raid the coasts from Vidim through the Donnermark and Krakova to northern Dornig. They have a culture of bear-shirted berserkers, who are especially fearsome. This berserker style has become popular with some of the younger dwarves of the cantons, with fighting competitions springing up that prize more savage combat.

Double strength level 4 wrecker [HUMANOID]
Initiative: +7

Great axe +12 vs. AC—28 damage

Dwarven fury: The dwarf's crit range expands by 1 and it makes an *overhead swing* attack as a quick action
Overhead swing +16 vs. AC—34 damage

   Limited use: Dwarven fury starts with one use per battle, and gains an extra use when the dwarf is first staggered.

   Battle scream: Whenever the dwarf scores a critical hit, its crit range expands by 2 but it loses 4 hit points.

   Dwarven tenacity: Ironcrag dwarves cannot be stunned, dazed or confused.

AC 20
PD 16   **HP 72**
MD 16

Dwarf Shieldbearer

They came forth banging their hammers on their shields and chanting songs of death and doom, and we believed them.

Level 4 mook [HUMANOID]
Initiative: +7

Hand axe +9 vs. AC—7 damage
  Natural 16+ hit or miss: Shield slam gains an extra use this battle.

Shield slam: When the dwarf is the target of a melee attack it rolls a save; on a success the attacker takes 3 damage and pops free.
  Limited use: Shield slam starts with one use per battle, and gains an extra use whenever the dwarf rolls a natural 16+ on an attack.

Dwarven tenacity: Ironcrag dwarves cannot be stunned, dazed or confused.

AC 20
PD 18   **HP 14 (mook)**
MD 14

Mook: Kill one dwarf shieldbearer mook for every 14 damage you deal to the mob.

Free Canton Mercenary

Many cantonal dwarves find ongoing employ in the armies of the Seven Cities and beyond. Clad in gleaming steel, dwarven soldiers often form the vanguard of important infantry forces, unleashing death from their heavy crossbows before charging with shields leading and axes held high.

Level 4 mook [HUMANOID]
Initiative: +7

War hammer +9 vs. AC—7 damage

R: Crossbow +9 vs. AC—7 damage
  Miss: Gain a +2 bonus to the next *crossbow* attack.

Dwarven tenacity: Ironcrag dwarves cannot be stunned, dazed or confused.

AC 20
PD 18   **HP 14 (mook)**
MD 14

Mook: Kill one free canton mercenary mook for every 14 damage you deal to the mob.

Free Canton Siegebreaker

Cantonal dwarves rank among the most war-tested dwarves in the world, for many rulers send envoys to the region to hire mercenaries. The dwarves do not fight for just anyone, though most powers surrounding the cantons have employed them at some time. Once confident in their borders' security and committed to a contract, however, these dwarves are bold and relentless. Many of these dour folk still sing the old songs and call upon Perun and Volund to strengthen their arms in battle. The mere sound of their arrival sometimes shakes the morale of lesser troops. Some human companies demand "dwarf pay" when forced to fight cantonal dwarves.

Level 5 troop [HUMANOID]
Initiative: +5

Sturdy battle axe +8 vs. AC—10 damage

R: Crossbow +8 vs. AC—10 damage

Shield Charge +8 vs. PD—8 damage and the next attack against the target by any dwarf does +8 damage.
  Natural 18+ hit: The dwarf makes a *sturdy battle axe* attack against the target as a quick action.

Dwarven tenacity: Ironcrag dwarves cannot be stunned, dazed or confused.

AC 22
PD 17   **HP 36**
MD 13

Ironcrag Marauder

One of the cantons' elite companies is the Ironcrag Marauders. Fierce and unpredictable, their view on life, the world, politics, and anything in between has been formed by years of seclusion in the mountains and below the rocky cliffs. Regardless of how they came to be involved in a given battle, those who face them are likely to meet a painful and often vicious death.

Double strength level 6 wrecker [HUMANOID]
Initiative: +18

Mountain hammer +14 vs. AC—38 damage
  Natural 16+ hit: The target is dazed (save ends).
  Natural 18+ hit or miss: The dwarf makes an *Ironcrag frenzy* attack as a quick action.

[Special trigger] **Ironcrag frenzy +14 vs. AC (1d3 enemies engaged with the dwarf)**—20 damage

Dwarven tenacity: Ironcrag dwarves cannot be stunned, dazed or confused.

AC 22
PD 20   **HP 130**
MD 16

ISONADE

More than a mere predator, the isonade is a beast of destruction, an agent of aggressive erosion. It wrecks seaside communities with battering winds and carves coastlines from below with its powerful magic. Though not very intelligent, sometimes the beast singles out a community and tries to lure residents into the waves by sending confused riddles, grand promises, and eerie noises with its whispering wind ability.

SECRETIVE CULT SACRIFICES

The hardy citizens of remote coastal communities are quick to blame hurricanes or tsunamis on the stirrings of the dreaded isonade. Some seek to appease the creature, and shadowy cults surround this monster. Most rumors of such worshipers describe a degenerate group seeking to draw the beast forth by sailing from sight of land and dumping a long chain of bound and screaming sacrifices into the lightless depths of the sea. Non-cultist citizens who learn of the sacrifices fear to speak out against them, effectively condoning the bloody practice by their silence.

ANCIENT AND TERRIBLE

Those ancient texts and rare individuals who describe the terrible creature say it weighs over 3 tons and reaches more than 45 feet from its gaping maw to the hooked fin of its wicked tail. The beast's age and origin remains unknown—many coastal cultures on Midgard have told tales of the isonade throughout their history.

MAGIC ITEMS

Hell's Heart Harpoon (heavy thrown weapon). Made of iron cooled in widows' tears. In addition to the usual item bonuses, you gain an additional +2 attack and damage bonus against aquatic enemies.

Once per battle: When you're fighting an individual enemy whom you've fought before, you can rally once during combat without having to make a save, for every time you've faced this foe previously. For example, if you've fought a particular dragon twice before, you can rally three times in combat against that dragon before you have to start making saves to rally. The next time you fight that dragon, you can rally four times.

Quirk: Never forget—nor forgive—those that have wronged you.

ADVENTURE HOOKS

Darkness in Shallow Waters: A small seaside fishing town has become reliant on outsiders spending their money there: all the fish are simply gone. But rumored sightings of an isonade are driving away visitors and townsfolk alike. In desperation the mayor hires the adventurers to investigate these rumors and, they're true, kill the beast or drive it away. But the mayor warns them to be discreet. If word gets out that the monster is real, and they fail to kill it, that will spell the end of the town.

Isonade

A gargantuan thrashing tail lined with cruelly hooked barbs shoots high into the air from beneath the waves, smashing all in its path and inundating the shoreline.

Huge level 10 wrecker [BEAST]
Initiative: +18

Swallow whole +15 vs. PD—30 damage and the target is swallowed (hard save ends). While swallowed, the target takes 30 acid damage at the end of its turn. The swallowed target can't see or affect anything but the isonade and other creatures swallowed by it. Likewise, anyone not swallowed by the isonade can't see or affect anyone inside the creature. If the target attacks the isonade using a close or ranged attack, on a miss it hits a random other creature swallowed by the isonade. When the effect ends, or the isonade drops to 0 hit points, the target appears in a spot of its choice nearby the isonade.

C: Bite +15 vs. AC (one nearby enemy)—60 damage and *underwater tremors* recharges
Natural 18+ hit: Tidal wave recharges.

C: Underwater tremors +15 vs. PD (1d3 nearby enemies)—180 damage and the target pops free
Miss: 90 damage.
Limited use: This ability can only be used once per battle, but recharges and can be used again this battle if the isonade succeeds on a *bite* attack.

R: Tidal wave +15 vs. PD (all nearby or far away enemies)—180 damage
Miss: 90 damage.
Hit or miss: Nearby buildings and structures suffer massive structural damage. Each building makes a save; if it fails it is flattened and/or washed away. Wooden structure = hard save, civilian brick or stone structure = normal save, fortified tower or wall = easy save. *All areas (both nearby and far away) become aquatic terrain until the end of the battle.* All non-aquatic enemies become hampered until they can climb onto floating debris or get to land (save ends).
Limited use: This ability can only be used once per battle, but recharges and can be used again this battle if the isonade succeeds on a *bite* attack with a natural 18+.

Sweeping tail: When an enemy misses the isonade with an attack it may immediately make the following attack as a quick action:
[Special trigger] **C: Sweeping tail +15 vs. AC (one nearby or far away enemy that just missed the isonade with an attack)**—60 damage

Deep sea dweller: The isonade can breathe underwater. In aquatic combat it gains a +2 bonus to attack rolls against non-aquatic creatures. The isonade can comfortably exist at any level of the sea and suffers no penalties at any depth. The isonade is slow and clumsy on land (-2 to hit) but very fast in the water. When it has to fight enemies on land it will use *tidal wave* to bring the water with it.

Lord of the sea: Whenever the isonade ends its turn, all dazed, stunned, or confused effects on it ends.

Whispering wind: The isonade may send a message on the wind (or waves, or water currents) of no more than 25 words to a designated spot within 20 miles. The whisper is as gentle and unnoticed as a zephyr until it reaches the location. It delivers its whisper-quiet message regardless of whether anyone is present to hear it. The wind (or wave, or current) then dissipates. It takes d20 minutes for the message to reach the spot.

AC 26
PD 24   **HP 650**
MD 20

KOBOLD GHETTO GUARD

The narrow, cramped streets of Zobeck give way to the even narrower streets of the Kobold Ghetto. Everything is made for kobold comfort, with no thought given to others. The streets are always dark as buildings lean into each other or the residents have thrown roofs over the cobblestones to let kobolds walk untroubled by rain or sunshine. Humans must squeeze through arches and alleys, and even a dwarf might brush his helmet against the top of a doorframe. The Ghetto has a rough reputation, and the kobold guards are part of the reason why.

SLIGHTLY BENT COPPERS

Most of Zobeck's kobolds are hardworking and industrious creatures that toil as miners, geargrinders, and clockworkers. Many build and repair the city's famed mechanical constructs. Others take up less scrupulous professions among Zobeck's thriving smuggling rings and thieves guilds.

The ghetto guards fall somewhere in between honest citizen and criminal element. They take bribes, pilfer some possessions as contraband, and shake down non-kobolds entering or leaving the Ghetto to supplement their wages. When real trouble kicks off, however, the ghetto guards come running or riding in on their giant owls and dire weasels. They might not bash the right heads, but some heads will definitely get bashed.

THINGS YOU MIGHT FIND ON A KOBOLD GHETTO GUARD...

Short length of rope. Lock picks (confiscated). Lock picks (official issue). Pencil stub and notebook (may contain incident reports, odds on local gambling events, maps of the ghetto or illegible scrawls). Half-brick in a sock. Hip flask of strong drink. Wooden truncheon, possibly made nastier by embedded metal or broken glass. Sturdy boots, good for kicking people when they are down. Chalk, for outlining bodies. Sharp knife, for making bodies. Wanted posters, nails, and a hammer. Helmet. Cheese. Dead mouse (a treat for a kobold mount perhaps). Dead mouse, covered in sweet honey batter (a kobold confectionary perhaps).

MORE THINGS YOU MIGHT FIND ON A KOBOLD GHETTO GUARD...

Badge. Spare boot laces. Silk handkerchief with lace edges, covered in dried snot. Wizard's wand, broken. Bag of tricks (see Kobold Owl Rider). Letter from the kobold's family back home. Letter of commendation from the kobold's superior. Letter of reprimand from the kobold's superior. Letter of resignation, undated, detailing the kobold guard's superior's many failings and detailed anatomical instructions on just what the kobold's superior can do with this job. Letter, purloined and potentially scandalous. Contraband. Half a gold piece, partially melted. Wooden spoon and mug. A silver dragon-head coin, a hole drilled through it and worn on a leather thong as a necklace. Gaol keys. Purse of low-denomination coins (about 1d8 sp in total) and some IOUs.

ADVENTURE HOOKS

Shocked! Shocked, I Say: The kobold guard have found themselves with a body they desperately need to get rid of. Their solution: drop it from above into the street in front of some adventurers, then "discover" the adventurers and arrest them for murder. Who was the corpse? Perhaps if the party can find that out, they can avoid kobold justice.

On The Case: The party wins a huge pile of loot from gambling. Kobolds steal the loot and disappear into the Ghetto. The kobolds all play deaf and dumb when the adventurers speak to them: nobody heard anything and nobody is willing to say anything. Fortunately (?) a kobold claiming to be a "Private Inquisitor" turns up offering to help, in exchange for a fee plus expenses. Can the kobold be trusted, or is this the next phase of a plan to relieve the too-talls of all their money?

Kobold Ghetto Guard

Blocking your passage into the Ghetto is a small group of officious-looking uniformed kobolds, searching potential troublemakers for contraband with a reckless disregard for personal property.

Level 0 troop [HUMANOID]
Initiative: +4

Too-tall catcher +5 vs. AC — 4 damage
Natural 16+: The target is grabbed. The kobold can only grab one creature at a time.

R: Clockwork crossbow +4 vs. AC — 4 damage

Nifty footwork: When a kobold misses with an attack it pops free of engagement.

Mob tactics: Kobold ghetto guards gain +1 to attack for every other kobold engaged with the target, up to a maximum of +4.

To me, my steed: An unmounted kobold dire weasel rider can summon its steed to it with a shouted command, if the dire weasel is within hearing distance. The dire weasel will arrive at the beginning of the kobold's next turn. The kobold can leap onto the dire weasel as a move action.

AC 16
PD 14
MD 10

HP 20

Dire Weasel

Large level 2 wrecker [BEAST]
Initiative: +7

Vicious Jaws +7 vs. AC — 14 damage
Natural 16+: The target is grabbed. The weasel can only grab one creature at a time. Grabbed creatures take 7 damage at the beginning of their turns.

Steed: Yes, some creatures can ride dire weasels. A small creature such as a kobold has no problems. A human would look ridiculous.

Mustelid frenzy: A staggered dire weasel gives its rider +2 damage bonus with melee attacks.

Keen scent: Dire weasels can scent (and attack with no penalty) nearby creatures who are invisible or hidden.

AC 18
PD 16
MD 12

HP 72

Kobold Guard Owl Rider

Level 0 archer [HUMANOID]
Initiative: +3

Spear +5 vs. AC— 4 damage

R: Clockwork Crossbow +4 vs. AC — 4 damage

Nifty footwork: When a kobold misses with an attack it pops free of engagement.

Death from above: On turns where the escalation die is odd the kobold can pull an item out of a bag and throw the item as a standard action.

R: Bag of tricks +4 vs. PD (one nearby or far away enemy) — roll d4 for effect:
1. Caltrops. Target takes 4 damage. For the rest of the battle anybody moving nearby where the caltrops fell must spend a standard action looking for caltrops or take 4 damage.
2. Alchemist's fire. 4 fire damage and 2 fire damage to all creatures nearby the target.
3. Chickenhead grenade. Target is covered in chicken gizzards and is stunned (easy save ends).
4. Flashbomb. Target takes 4 damage and is dazed (save ends).

To me, my steed: An unmounted kobold owl rider on open ground can summon its steed to it with a shouted command, if the giant owl is within hearing distance. The giant owl will arrive at the beginning of the kobold's next turn. The kobold can hoist itself onto the owl as a move action.

AC 16
PD 14   **HP 20**
MD 10

Giant Owl

Level 1 troop [BEAST]
Initiative: +7

Swooping Claws +6 vs. AC— 5 damage
Natural even roll: The owl pops free of engagement and can move as a free action.

Steed: A small creature (such as a kobold) can ride a giant owl.

Weave and bob: Owls give their riders +2 to AC.

I am death, a winged beast: Giant owls can fly, silently and swiftly. They are deadly predators, and can see at night. While they can swoop and fly unerringly through cluttered city streets or tangled branches, they cannot hover.

AC 18
PD 16   **HP 72**
MD 12

Kobold Ghetto Guard Sergeant

Level 1 troop [HUMANOID]
Initiative: +4

Sergeant's mace +6 vs. AC— 5 damage
Natural even hit: Target is dazed (save ends).

R: Clockwork crossbow +5 vs. AC — 5 damage

"Keep going lads!": As a quick action the kobold ghetto guard sergeant grants all nearby allies 5 hit points.

Nifty footwork: When a kobold misses with an attack it pops free of engagement.

To me, my steed: An unmounted kobold dire weasel rider can summon its steed to it with a shouted command, if the dire weasel is within hearing distance. The dire weasel will arrive at the beginning of the kobold's next turn. The kobold can leap onto the dire weasel as a move action.

AC 17
PD 15   **HP 27**
MD 11

LICH HOUND

Half bone, half dark purple fire, lich hounds are creatures of hunger and the hunt. They have white skulls, massive bone bodies (far heavier and thicker than a normal dog's bones), and powerful heavy jaws. Their eyes burn green or blue, and their tongues resemble black fire.

LOYAL TO DARK MASTERS

Made of necromantic power, these hounds serve ghoul high priests and arch-liches. With their powerful senses and a keen ability to find the living they are expert trackers, and relentlessly hunt their prey. Lich hound howls fade into and out of normal hearing, with strangely shifting pitch and echoes.

Lich hounds always arrive wreathed in mist. They tear down creatures larger than themselves or race through the air to catch a surprised bat in mid-flight. All cruelty and fangs, they live for the hunt and for praise from their undead lords.

FROM BONE TO SPIRIT

As the great hunt continues, the body of the lich hound breaks down and fades away, though this hardly slows the foul beast. They emerge as spectral wolves and, unburdened by physical forms, grow in strength as they learn new tactics. The eternal hunt becomes more important to these spirits, and their undead masters sometimes lose direct control. Free spectral wolves sometimes work with shamans or form packs with other hungering undead, such as ghouls and wraiths.

PACK FIGHTERS

Lich hounds fight in groups and always use their howl to attempt to shake the morale of their victims. If that fails, they aid one another in attacking a single foe, trying to trip him and drag him down for a gut ripping attack. The spectral wolf prefers to let any non-wolf allies attack first. It then either sneaks or teleports into combat and attacks the wounded. It focuses on an injured target until others start to surround it and then uses it's abilities to pass through unearthly realms to escape and reach a new, more isolated target.

MAGIC ITEMS

Lich-Bone Bow (any bow or crossbow). This weapon made from the bones of a lich hound becomes ghostly in strong light. You may use this bow while engaged to make ranged attacks without provoking attacks of opportunity.

Once per day: As a move action you can become temporarily ghostly and teleport to wherever your arrow or bolt lands, regaining your corporeal form at your destination.

Quirk: Gnaw on the bones of your fallen enemies.

ADVENTURE HOOKS

Curse and Cause: For the last five nights a rural village has been plagued by eerie howling. Any who attempt to leave town are killed by unknown assailants as soon as they set foot in the woods. The adventurers are the first outsiders to arrive in several days, and the villagers immediately turn to them for help. Lich hounds are stalking the woods, but something prevents them from coming into the village. Why are they here, and what's keeping them away?

The Window of Fear: A cleric approaches the party about strange doings in his small shrine: an acolyte died interrupting a midnight ritual by an unknown spellcaster. In a past age, a hero magically trapped a pack of spectral wolves in the shrine's glass windows. During the night, those inside the shrine hear an unearthly howling and see the wolves through the windows—but when they step outside there's no howling, and no wolves to be seen. Is someone trying to free the pack? For what purpose?

Lich Hound

As the cloud of smoky shadow dissipates you see that this vile hound is in a state of partial decomposition. It lunges for you amid the chilling howls of its fellows.

Level 3 troop [UNDEAD]
Initiative: +9
Vulnerable: holy

Soulrender Bite +8 vs. PD—10 negative energy damage

Night howl: Against living foes, the lich hound's crit range expands by 2 (crits on 18+).

Into the shadows: On rounds where the escalation die is odd the lich hound may teleport to any point nearby or far away. If the lich hound is in shadows or darkness when it teleports, the move doesn't provoke attacks.

Lifesense: The hound is aware of living nearby or far away creatures, and is immune to the effects of *invisiblity*, *blur* and other magical attempts to conceal or disguise the presence of the living.

Feast of entrails: As a free action when a nearby or far away enemy fails a death save, the lich hound immediately teleports so that it is engaged with the dying enemy and does 6 negative energy damage to the target.

Resist negative energy 11+: When a negative energy attack targets this creature, the attacker must roll a natural 11+ on the attack roll or it only deals half damage.

AC 19
PD 17   **HP 45**
MD 11

Spectral Wolf

You hear them long before they materialize, their unearthly howls echoing throughout the woods.

Level 4 troop [UNDEAD]
Initiative: +12
Vulnerable: holy

Ghost bite +9 vs. AC—14 damage (18 damage if the target is hampered).

Press the advantage: When the wolf successfully attacks an enemy that is engaged with an ally, the target is hampered (save ends).

Otherworldly jaunt: The wolf may teleport to any spot nearby as a move action. If it isn't engaged with enemies at the end of the movement the wolf becomes invisible (+5 to defenses). The invisibility ends when it next attacks or at the end of its next turn.

Resist negative energy 11+: When a negative energy attack targets this creature, the attacker must roll a natural 11+ on the attack roll or it only deals half damage.

AC 20
PD 15   **HP 54**
MD 17

MAGES OF ALLAIN

No humans take magic more seriously than the arcanists of Allain. These mages are inheritors of the last great magocracy, the survivor of an escalating mage war that called forth the eldritch horrors that created the Western Wastes. Spellcasters populate these lands in great numbers, pursuing their own arcane schemes and ensnaring others in their plots. Strange offers abound, and mysteriously hooded strangers beckon from the dark corners of nearly every inn and tavern. Little is known about these strange arcanists; their humanity is suspect, but their great power is unquestioned. Arrogant and cruel, the wizards care little for the lives of the last magocracy's citizens beyond their use in experiments and dark machinations.

R. HERSHEY

ELDRITCH PATRONS

Whether retrieving some lost artifact or gathering information on the blasphemous horrors in the wastes, few of the adventurous, foolhardy, or desperate who accept a mage's commission collect their payment. Despite the dangers, prospective clients rarely refuse these offers. Perhaps dark magic causes them to follow the wizard's instruction. More likely, though, the slim chance of survival—as opposed to the certain doom of refusing the job—motivates the hirelings.

THINGS YOU MIGHT FIND ON A MAGE OF ALLAIN...

Hooded cowl. Crystalline rod. Richly embroidered robe. Keys suspended from a charm bracelet. Twisted bonewood staff. Tattoos of intricate star charts and calculation tables. Tattoos of exploding runes! (Take 12 points damage.) Tattoos of a contract with an eldritch abomination, portions dance and smudge when anybody tries to read them. Crystal orb. A pouch of sand, worn under the robes next to the mage's skin. Champion tier healing potion. Walking cane with concealed sword. 3d6 runes ready to be applied to a weapon or armor. Pouch of coins that explodes if taken more than two moves beyond the mage's person without a control word being said first (18 damage to all nearby creatures).

REAGENTS YOU MIGHT FIND ON A MAILLON ALCHEMIST...

Moon Tears (smelly, turns blue when gold is dipped into it). Nirolex's Elixir (eye-watering non-smell). Zetuvit's Distillation (cloudy, stains stone red). Unwater of Maillon (makes you thirsty if drunk at midnight, otherwise acts much like normal water). Princess' Water (smells of roses and regret). Powder of Akiontite (skin irritant). Polymath's Lament (a dried grass). A gram of Mercurial Splendor (priceless or worthless depending on who you ask). Sunsand (glows in moonlight). Regia Pulvis (a dust, it makes fire flare unusual colors). Cerae Mortis (a crumbly waxy substance, it smells awful). Monarch's Oil (made from the poison of the deadly butterfly, only harmful in very large quantities).

MAGIC ITEMS

Mantle of The Arcanist (cloak). The richly embroidered hood hides your features. *Once per day:* As a free action regain the use of an expended daily spell. If it is the last spell you cast you may choose to recast it immediately as a quick action with a -2 penalty to hit.

Quirk: Cackle instead of laugh.

Cloak of Desert Night (cloak). The thin silk cloak seems translucent yet it perfectly obscures your features. *Recharge 16+:* As a move action you briefly transform into a whirling dust-cloud and teleport to anywhere nearby or far away that dust could get into. It is obvious to observers in which direction you have travelled.

Quirk: Incessant thirst.

Transmuter's Staff (staff - weapon/implement). A twisted length of acid-scarred wood, with glyphs burnt into it. You may forgo miss damage and instead transform your target into a tree. The target is rooted to the ground (stuck) and may only make basic attacks with its limbs (hampered). A successful save ends both conditions and turns the target back to its normal form.

Quirk: You are interested in the biology of your companions, and how it might be "improved."

Blackheart Staff (staff - weapon/implement). An expensive looking black staff inlaid with silver and copper. Each attack that includes an ally as a target expands your crit range by 1 for the rest of the battle.

Quirk: Paranoid about what others are planning to do to you while you sleep.

ADVENTURE HOOKS

Collateral Damage: Two rival houses of arcanists are constantly bickering and fighting and it has lately turned deadly. To prevent the assembled wizards, warpcasters, alchemists, and reality-weavers from going to war with each other a wise magister has devised a plan for a proxy war, and had both houses agree to it: Whichever house can best ruin the party's lives (without outright killing them) shall be declared the superior house.

The Great Snipe Hunt: The alchemists of Maillon have created a wondrous new creature - a thing of unsurpassed beauty and power which unfortunately vanished. In actuality the beast was nothing more than a hallucination brought on by alchemical fumes and unstable magic. Nonetheless the mages are convinced that it was real and pay the adventurers to find it and bring it back. Rival alchemists, who have been trying for years to create life, will stop at nothing to make sure that the adventurers do not find the wondrous beast.

The Tintager Irregulars: A band of brave young apprentices wish to prove themselves by patrolling for 'elven incursions'. They hire the adventurers as guides and set out for the elven forests. Young hot-heads with magic storming off into unknown lands with the party in tow—what could go wrong?

TATTOOED ADEPTS

The wizards of the city of Bemmea are known masters of glyph magic, and several carry their entire repertoire of spells tattooed on their skin (despite prohibitions against ink magic). These mystic scrawls allow the wizards to recall spent magics and to cast their spells faster than their opponents.

Although they often appear as solitary figures, hooded and cloaked against the prying daylight, Bemmean wizards are never truly alone. Most have bound a small number of invisible sand devils from the wastes into service. These creatures skulk near their masters at all times, ready to defend them against attackers.

INVISIBLE SERVANTS

The invisible sand devils, properly named haborgoi, arose during the magical turmoil of the Great Mage War. As powerful arcanists dueled over the ley lines of western Midgard, they caused terrible damage to the land. They warped nature and gave rise to all manner of strange creatures and unnatural phenomena. The sand devils rose up out of the aftermath of the devastation and rampaged across the blasted landscape.

An archmage of Bemmea named Tajenfer of the Cowled Visage first developed the ritual to bind the haborgoi to protect him from his rivals. When Tajenfer destroyed four of his enemies without lifting a finger, binding sand devils became all the rage among the wizards of Bemmea's Academies Arcana.

Bemmean Wizard

The sinister, hooded figure sitting across from you exudes an aura of equal parts power and arrogance.

Level 7 caster [HUMANOID]
Initiative: +14

Staff +12 vs. AC—28 force damage

Shrivel limb +12 vs. AC (wizard must be wielding its staff)—24 negative energy damage
Natural 16+ hit: The target is stuck until the end of its next turn.

R: Visions of things that should not be +12 vs. PD—24 psychic damage and the target is dazed (save ends).
Natural odd hit: The target takes an extra 14 psychic damage and is stunned (save ends).

R: The doom below +12 vs. PD (1d3 nearby or far away enemies in a group)—20 force damage and the target is transported into another dimension (easy save ends). While removed from this reality the target can continue to make saves against ongoing effects, but does not take ongoing damage. Failed death or last gasp saves do not count towards the number of failed saves. Once a creature has returned from the other dimension, saves and ongoing damage resume normally and it is immune to *the doom below* for the rest of the battle.

R: Black geas +12 vs. MD—The wizard causes a magical tattoo to appear somewhere on the target's body. This tattoo compels the target to take no actions (save ends). The target may ignore this compulsion, but if so the target takes 14 damage and is thrown about the battlefield (the wizard repositions the target somewhere nearby the target's original position).

Limited use: Only one person may have the *black geas* tattoo at a time. If the attack hits, the attack cannot be used again until the target succeeds on a save against the *black geas*.

Arcane shield: Once per round when an enemy hits the wizard with an attack, the wizard gains +4 to AC and PD until the end of its next turn. When an *arcane shield* is in place, the wizard can choose to make a *black geas* or *the doom below* attack as a free action at any time, even outside of its normal turn. Doing so ends the *arcane shield* and removes the bonuses.

AC 23
PD 19   **HP 108**
MD 23

Invisible Sand Devil
A faint whispering sound is all you can detect.

Level 5 troop [DEMON]
Initiative: +10

Sand blast +13 vs. AC—15 damage

C: Cloud of sand +8 vs. PD (1d3 nearby targets)—12 damage and the target is weakened (save ends).

Limited use: Once per battle, but *cloud of sand* recharges and can be used again if the sand devil goes a round without being hit.

Sweep all aside: As a move action the sand devil flies to a spot nearby and pulls 1d3 nearby enemies into engagement with it. If *cloud of sand* hasn't been expended, the sand devil can make a *cloud of sand* attack against those enemies as a quick action.

Invisibility: The sand devil is nearly invisible (this is already accounted for in its defenses). Enemies who can perceive invisible creatures gain +3 to hit the sand devil with attacks that target AC.

AC 24
PD 22   **HP 42**
MD 12

MISGUIDED DEFENDERS OF TINTAGER
The city of Tintager accepts all who come to serve on the border and guard against intrusion from the elves of Arbonesse, meaning outcasts from elsewhere can find acceptance here. Horned and fanged tiefling warmages are a common sight, often culled from the ranks of Bemmea's failed apprentices and hardened in conflict and war.

Despite the "elven aggression" Tintager's officials always mention, Arbonesse soldiers rarely cross the border. More commonly, the warmages of Tintager invade elven territory to claim decades-old bounties on elven outlaws, test elven defenses, or accompany expeditions to fell entire groves of trees and ship their trunks back to Maillon for alchemical preparation. Despite the elves' reluctance to retaliate, the warmages stay busy with frequent scuffles with goblins and aberrations from the wastes.

Like their Bemmean counterparts, Tintager's warmages favor hooded robes to conceal their inhuman features. From time to time, a warmage will discreetly hire adventurous individuals to go with them into the elven forests for his own nefarious purposes, which the mage will rarely makes clear to their companions.

Warmage of Tintager
Spoiling for a fight, looking for a war.

Level 6 caster [HUMANOID]
Initiative: +11

Cold iron longsword +11 vs. AC—21 damage

R: Blackfire blood bolt +11 vs. PD—12 damage and 7 ongoing negative energy damage.

Natural even hit: 14 ongoing psychic damage and the target is weakened (easy save ends both).

Arcane shield: Once per round when an enemy hits the warmage with an attack, the warmage gains +4 to AC and PD until the end of its next turn. When an *arcane shield* is in place, the warmage can choose to make a *blackfire blood bolt* attack as a free action at any time, even outside of its normal turn. Doing so ends the *arcane shield* and removes the bonuses.

Elf slayer: The warmage does an extra 6 points of damage against elves and other fey creatures.

AC 22
PD 16   **HP 90**
MD 20

UNCHECKED EXPERIMENTATION IN MAILLON

The alchemists of Allain live a chaotic but prosperous existence in the ramshackle buildings and rickety houseboats of the sinking city of Maillon. Banished by the Ninemage Council following the Great Mage War, the alchemists built a city in the swamp where they could collect strange plants and outlandish ingredients, and pursue their dangerous experiments. Their laissez-faire attitude toward pollution means that alchemical waste usually ends up in the waters below this city built on stilts, often leading to the inadvertent creation of warped wildlife, alchemical oozes, and worse. The alchemists do a brisk trade in potions, elixirs, and drugs. They sometimes enlist the aid of outsiders in obtaining hard-to-find components. Many alchemists have been affected in strange ways by exposure to their own concoctions.

Maillon Alchemist

Do you smell that? Either a toxic chemical dump is nearby, or a Maillon alchemist.

Level 6 caster [HUMANOID]
Initiative: +12

Alchemist's staff +11 vs. AC—28 damage
> *Natural 18+ hit or miss:* One non-magical item belonging to the target turns to lead and the target is weakened (save ends).
> *Natural 1 hit or miss:* One non-magical item belonging to the target turns to gold and the target can take a recovery.

R: Acid splash +11 vs. PD—21 acid damage and the target is stunned until the end of the alchemist's next turn.
> *Natural 18+ hit or miss:* The alchemist makes a *chymical explosion* attack.

[Special trigger] C: Chymical explosion +11 vs. PD (1d3 enemies nearest to *acid splash* target)—14 poison damage and the target is dazed (save ends).
> *Miss:* 7 poison damage.

C: Incandescent spray +11 vs. PD (1d3 nearby enemies in a group)—21 force damage and 7 ongoing fire damage
> *Hit or miss:* Any nearby enemy who is already taking ongoing fire damage takes 7 fire damage.

C: Writhing Arms +11 vs AC—28 damage and the target is stuck and weakened until the end of the alchemist's next turn, as the alchemist's arms momentarily turn into writing tentacles and lash out.
> *Natural 18+ hit or miss:* One healing potion carried by the target is permanently (and obviously) transformed into poison appropriate to the target's tier.
> *Natural 1 hit or miss:* One non-magical liquid carried by the target is permanently (and obviously) transformed into a healing potion appropriate to the target's tier.
> *Limited Use:* Once per battle.

AC 22
PD 16 **HP 90**
MD 19

MERROW

Merrow are river trolls that haunt the waterways and estuaries of Midgard, seeking to consume the freshly drowned. These large, humanoid creatures of fey origin have tough pebbled hide in shades of dark green and blue, and webbed feet and hands. Their long, straggly black hair often carries bits of seaweed and river moss, and they adorn themselves with the bones of humans or other intelligent land dwellers.

EXILED TO THE RIVERS

Driven out of their ancestral homelands in the depths of the oceans by the hated merfolk, merrow resent the living they have scratched out for themselves in the shallow inland rivers. Encountered as either solitary hunters or in small bands, merrow have a loose-knit tribal society led by a local shaman or slaughter priest. They live only to feed and offer the entrails of their victims to the forgotten aboleth gods of the sea.

STRIKE FROM THE SHADOWS

Retaining vestiges of their lost civilization, merrow rarely fight with tooth and claw like other trolls. They prefer to use the trident and net of their ancestors. They recognize that their numbers are few, however, and often seek to strike from ambush or under cover of darkness to assure themselves easy victories, and use their teleportation power to appear unexpectedly. Some merrow make their homes near the haunt of other aquatic monsters, where they can scavenge and feed on the scraps left over from helpless victims.

THINGS YOU MIGHT FIND ON A MERROW…

Fish-skull good luck charm. Goblin shark tooth necklace. Turtle-shell armor. Stinking loincloth. Unholy symbol. Net. Shirt made like a net. Nose ring. Earrings. Scrap of leather on which is a depiction of a foul aboleth-god. Pieces of scavenged armor.

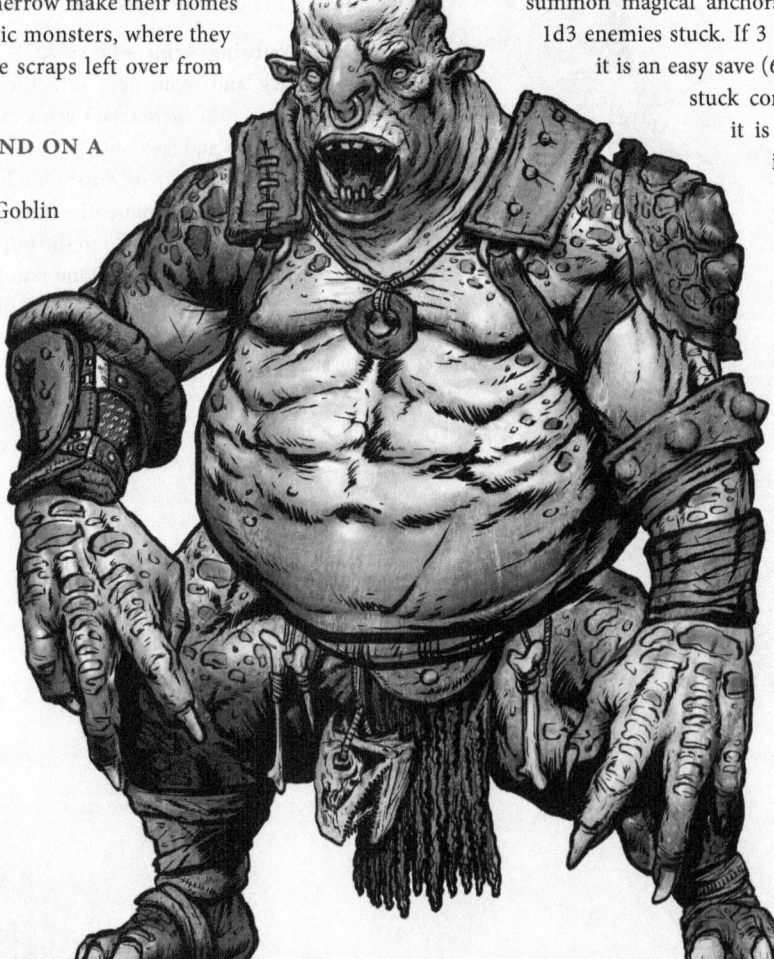

MAGIC ITEMS

Foulwater Totem (holy symbol). A twisted circular braid of seaweed and river reeds, with dried fish guts running through it. *Recharge 16+:* As a quick action you may command the spirits controlled by the totem to flood the area. The area that the battle is in floods, making it an aquatic environment for the remainder of the battle. All non-aquatic enemies must save or become stuck (save ends) on rounds where the escalation die is odd.

Quirk: You like to lurk. Whether it's in the shadows, in a corner, or on the edges of a gathering, you're there. Lurking.

Trident of the Abyss (trident, light or heavy two-handed melee). Nobody knows what deep-sea creature wrought this twisted length of metal. On a critical hit resolve the attack as normal, and your target becomes vulnerable to your attacks for the rest of the battle as they start to drown in a globe of crushing deep-sea water that envelops their head. If your enemy is aquatic or doesn't need to breathe then save ends the vulnerable condition.

Quirk: You smell of decaying fish.

Tidestrand Trident (trident, heavy two-handed melee). This three-pronged weapon was washed ashore after a tragic shipwreck. *Recharge 16+:* As a quick action summon magical anchors and chains to make 1d3 enemies stuck. If 3 enemies become stuck it is an easy save (6+) for each to end the stuck condition; if 2 are stuck it is a normal save (11+); if only 1 is stuck it is a hard save (16+).

Quirk: Obsession with shipwrecks and other disasters.

ADVENTURE HOOKS

12 Angry Merrow: The adventurers encounter a band of merrow who, surprisingly, have no interest in fighting them—they're on a different errand. Their slaughter priest was recently killed, but not for food or pleasure (which the merrow would understand). Instead it was killed by a wizard who took its body for spell components. The slaughter priest needs to be properly laid to rest. Will the adventurers join the merrow, or side with the wizard?

Merrow

Resembling a troll, this creature has pebbled skin, lank and briny hair, and webbed hands and feet.

Level 4 troop [HUMANOID]
Initiative: +12

Masterwork trident +9 vs. AC—14 damage

Surprising reach: The merrow may choose to make this attack as a close attack against one nearby target instead of as a melee attack.

R: Hurl trident +9 vs. AC—14 damage

C: Lure of the wild +9 vs. MD (one nearby enemy)—Target pops free and is pulled into engagement with the merrow. Afterward the merrow may immediately make a *masterwork trident* attack against the target as a quick action.
Miss: 5 psychic damage.
Limited use: Once per battle.

Vicious skirmisher: On the first turn the merrow is engaged with a target the merrow does +7 damage on a hit or a miss.

Aquatic: The merrow can breathe under water just as well as it breathes air, and is an expert swimmer. It gains +2 to hit and damage with all attacks when fighting a non-aquatic foe in an aquatic environment.

Mist walker: Once per battle the merrow can teleport to any point nearby that it can see as a move action. After it does so it may make an attack as a quick action.

Watery grave: Once per day a merrow can make the water covering the ground in an area (such as a shoreline, a river, or a flooded corridor) rise up, making the area an aquatic environment. *Watery grave* cannot take effect where water does not cover the ground.

AC 20
PD 18   **HP 54**
MD 17

Merrow Slaughter Priest

It is said they still pray to their deep aboleth gods, even after all this time...

Level 5 caster [HUMANOID]
Initiative: +13

Masterwork trident +10 vs. AC—18 damage

Surprising reach: The merrow may choose to make this attack as a close attack against one nearby target instead of as a melee attack.

R: Hurl trident +10 vs. AC—18 damage

R: Rainwild river jet +10 vs. PD—18 damage

Natural 14+ hit: Include a second enemy in the attack, using the same attack roll.
Natural 16+ hit: Include a third enemy in the attack, using the same attack roll.
Natural 18+ hit or miss: Each enemy takes 5 ongoing damage.
Natural odd hit or miss: Target is hampered (save ends).

Aquatic: The merrow can breathe under water just as well as it breathes air, and is an expert swimmer. It gains +2 to hit and damage with all attacks when fighting a non-aquatic foe in an aquatic environment.

Mist walker: Once per battle the merrow teleports to any point nearby or far away as a move action. After it does so it may make an attack as a quick action.

Watery grave: Once per day a merrow can make the water covering the ground in an area (such as a shoreline, a river, or a flooded corridor) rise up, making the area an aquatic environment. *Watery grave* cannot take effect where water does not cover the ground.

AC 21
PD 16   **HP 72**
MD 18

MHAROTI DRAGONKIN

Dragonkin have small, supple, burnished scales covering their dragon-like faces, hands, and chest, but larger and more rigid scales on their backs, shoulders, and forearms. Most dragonkin have grey, brown, tan, gold, silver, or black scales; a rare few have reddish-orange, greenish-yellow, or star-like blue and black scales.

All dragonkin have clawed hands and feet, and their faces are dominated by short snouts, with black or gold eyes. Males are larger and horned or crested, and considerably heavier than females. Their tails are short and often spiked. Female dragonkin are smaller, faster, and wiry, with longer, lashing tails. They sometimes have a frill or collar of contrasting color.

Dragonkin wear armor, for their scales are only slightly more protective than human or dwarvish skin. All dragonkin are heavy and slow for their size, but they also seem to exude a certain commanding presence and sense of destiny that most humanoid races find appealing.

CHILDREN OF THE EMPIRE

The Mharoti dragonkin consider themselves the scions of the Dragon Empire. Though their origins remain lost to time, dragonkin have long served as the lair guardians and brood servants of the eastern dragons. As the empire grew, and the dragons' power expanded, the dragonkin found new roles as the empire's shock troops, paladins, and sorcerers. Though somewhat rare outside the empire, unless on official business, a few dragonkin appear throughout the south and east of Midgard.

A SHOW OF RESPECT

The sultana occasionally sends her elemental priests and magic-users as diplomats and trade negotiators, though negotiation is a relative concept to emissaries backed by the might of the empire. Always spellcasters, these dragonkin can, supposedly, communicate with their masters from anywhere in Midgard. Ever accompanied by their kilij-bearing bodyguards, Mharoti emissaries take little notice of those they consider below their station, which includes non-noble humans and all dwarves and minotaurs. Emissaries prefer to rely on their magic and bodyguards in battle but are skilled in the use of their iron runestaves, status symbols among the more martial elemental cults of the east.

DEFENDERS OF THE DRAGON LORDS

Some of the oldest and most powerful dragonkin are rarely seen by outsiders or even other Mharoti citizens, for they have the great honor of directly serving of one of the twenty dragon lords. Secreted away to their dragon's lair, these scaled champions master their martial practices and elemental magic away from prying eyes.

The practice of the draconic elemental arts rises to new heights in these chambers. Elemental scions command each element in surprising ways, shrouding their claws in chilling fire, blinding enemies with smoke, or summoning earthen chains to bind and crush their opponents.

R. HERSHEY -11

THINGS YOU MIGHT FIND ON A MHAROTI DRAGONKIN...

Scimitar. Iron staff. Sleeveless leather coat. Metal breastplate. Robes. Dragon-helm. Scale armor. Vambraces made of bone softened in dragon fire. Halberd. Amulet depicting the elements in dynamic harmony. Scale-wax (for giving scales a healthy sheen). Purse of gold pieces shaped like claws (10+d20 gp). Flask of strong drink. Broad leather belt with slim metal boxes affixed to the outside, each box contains a useful item (possibilities include: silk rope and folding grapple, handcuffs and set of keys, bandages impregnated with healing balm that adds 1d8 to hit points recovered, single-use alchemical light, small sharp knife with unfolding utility tools useful for fixing clockwork or removing food from between dragonkin teeth).

MAGIC ITEMS

Ring of Dragonkind (ring). This signet ring is made of bands of silver and gold that shifts about on the finger.

Once per day: When not taking part in a battle, you may sprout draconic wings and fly for five minutes.

Recharge 16+: You may manifest wings in combat, but only briefly. When you are missed by a melee attack you may pop free of all enemies engaged with you and move as a free action. *Quirk:* Certain of your own absolute superiority.

Iron-Star Staff (staff - weapon/implement). A unadorned staff of dense iron that warps the light around it. If your attack does fire damage, change the result of your lowest damage die result to be the maximum it could have rolled. If your attack does not do fire damage, you may change the attack type to fire (but that attack doesn't get the damage-die advantage.) *Quirk:* Pyromania.

ADVENTURE HOOKS

Murder Most Heated: A dragonkin bathhouse serves as a home away from home for visiting Mharoti. Unfortunately three scribes have been found dead, face down in a bath of steaming salt-water with daggers in their backs implicating a rival power. The local authorities need an uninterested third party to investigate the dragonkin and uncover what they know.

The Spiral: A caravan of dragonkin were escorting a wagon containing a dragon egg to Bratislor, to seal an agreement between the undead who rule from Bratis Castle and the Sultana. Disaster struck when bandits attacked and stole the wagon, and drove off with it. The frantic dragonkin set aside their haughtiness and seek the adventurers' help recovering the wagon (provided the adventurers don't ask what is inside it).

Mharoti Dragonkin Guard

As the dragonkin shifts its weight and its hand moves purposefully towards its kilij you realize that the joke you just made about the dragon and the barmaid was ill-timed.

Level 4 troop [HUMANOID]
Initiative: +12

Kilij scimitar +9 vs. AC—14 damage
Natural 16+ hit: Ongoing 5 damage.

Parry and claw: When an enemy that the dragonkin is engaged with makes a melee attack that does not include the dragonkin, it may make a *parry and claw* attack against that enemy as an immediate free action.

Parry and Claw +8 vs. Value of the triggering attack roll—7 damage
Natural odd hit: The triggering attack does half damage to its target.
Natural even hit: The triggering attack does no damage to its target.
Natural 18+ hit: The target of the *claw* attack is vulnerable to the dragonkin guard's attacks for the rest of the battle.

Night vision: The dragonkin can see as well in non-magical darkness as it does in daylight.

AC 20
PD 15   **HP 54**
MD 16

Mharoti Dragonkin Emissary

Casting off its hood the Mharoti emissary reveals its true, draconic nature as it charges its iron staff with arcane fire.

Level 5 caster [HUMANOID]
Initiative: +12

Staff of iron +10 vs. AC—10 damage
Natural odd hit: 20 fire damage.

R: Thunderbolt +10 vs. PD—18 thunder damage
Natural odd hit: Target becomes vulnerable to all attacks (save ends).

Ignite iron: As a quick action the emissary can enchant its weapon or the weapon of a nearby ally. The weapon deals +6 fire damage, and does 5 ongoing fire damage on a critical hit. The emissary can dismiss this effect as a free action. The enchantment can only be on one weapon at a time.

Healing touch: As a quick action the emissary may heal itself or one nearby ally for 10 hit points.
Limited use: Once per battle.

Flight: The emissary can fly a short distance using magic. It must land at the end of its move or fall.

AC 21
PD 16   **HP 72**
MD 18

Mharoti Dragonkin Sentinel

The Mharoti smirks as it expertly spins its halberd in a complex pattern. Then it crooks one clawed finger, beckoning you to come closer.

Level 8 troop [HUMANOID]
Initiative: +17

Halberd +13 vs. AC—30 damage

Natural 16+ hit: Include a second enemy in the attack, using the same attack roll.

Natural 18+ hit: Include a third enemy in the attack, using the same attack roll.

Natural odd hit: Target is dazed (easy save ends).

Thrust: The dragonkin may choose to make this attack as a close attack against one nearby target instead of as a melee attack, but gains no bonus for rolling 16+ or 18+.

Parry and trip: When a nearby enemy that the dragonkin makes a melee attack that does not include the dragonkin, it may make a *parry and trip* attack against that enemy as an immediate free action.

Parry and trip +10 vs. Value of the triggering attack roll—12 damage

Natural odd hit: The triggering attack does half damage to its target.

Natural even hit: The triggering attack does no damage to its target.

Natural 18+ hit: The target of the *parry and trip* attack is dazed (save ends).

Dragon blood rage: Whenever the sentinel is staggered (at 72 hit points or less) it takes a -1 penalty to attack rolls but gains a +5 bonus to damage rolls. On a critical hit, it also does an extra 10 ongoing damage.

AC 24
PD 19   **HP 144**
MD 18

Mharoti Dragonkin Elemental Scion

The dust whirls around the Mharoti's feet as it hovers an inch above the ground. Lightning jumps between its hands and a nimbus of fire glows around its head.

Level 9 caster [HUMANOID]
Initiative: +16

Mystical claw +14 vs. AC—40 cold damage

Natural 16+ hit: 10 ongoing fire damage.

Natural 18+ hit or miss: The mharoti may make an *arcane chains* attack this turn as a quick action.

R: Thunderbolt +14 vs. PD—50 thunder damage

Natural 16+ hit: Target becomes hampered (easy save ends).

Natural 18+ hit or miss: The mharoti may make an *arcane chains* attack this turn as a quick action.

C: Arcane chains +14 vs. PD (one nearby enemy)—10 force damage and the target is stuck (save ends)

Puff of smoke: Once per battle as a quick action; the mharoti casts a spell to create an area of darkly roiling magical smoke around one nearby or far away creature or object. Any creature nearby the creature or object affected takes a -4 penalty to its ranged attacks and gains a +4 bonus to defenses against ranged attacks. Creatures that can see through magical darkness or who do not need to see to fight are unaffected by the penalty to attack. The effect lasts until the end of the battle, even if the mharoti is slain. The effect can be dispelled by a sufficiently powerful wind or any magic that dispels magical effects.

Robe of winds: Any creature that ends its turn engaged with the mharoti pops free.

AC 25
PD 20   **HP 180**
MD 23

MINOTAUR

A race of proud warriors, minotaurs enjoy confusing their enemies with an ever shifting battlefield. They charge and fall back, move swiftly for their size, and take every advantage offered by the terrain.

Both sexes have horned heads covered with shaggy hair. Warriors often braid this hair with teeth or other tokens of fallen enemies. The thick hair covering their large bodies can vary widely from bright white to medium red-browns to dark brown and black. Many shave or dye their fur in patterns signifying their allegiances and beliefs. Other decorations include brands and ritual scars. Minotaurs prize their horns and love to adorn and carve them with runes commemorating great accomplishments. This makes their horns a combination of personal history, natural weapon, and symbol of knowledge visible to any who know how to read.

AT HOME WHERE NEEDED

Minotaurs make their homes throughout Midgard, but the vast majority live on the Isle of Kyprion or in the city of Kaptaria, in the Barony of Capleon. While both communities favor brute strength and glory in combat, Kaptarians pride themselves on holding tightly to ancient minotaur values. Unable to find glory in their traditional homes, many minotaurs leave every year. Some have suffered a broken horn and seek to prove themselves worthy of their blood. Others dedicate themselves to learning, often by visiting the great mazes of the world. The rest find employment as sailors, gladiators, bodyguards, and the like.

Nobility and successful merchants favor minotaur bodyguards. These protectors train so they can read the body movements of their enemies and give their protectees instructions to avoid attacks. When their protection fails, they charge in to deliver a devastating blow. The minotaurs of Kyprion are justly famed for their prowess as sailors, and many of these fierce islanders find it only natural to combine the two pursuits. Vassals to the seafaring nation of Triolo, Kyprion marines are prized members of any ship's crew and are typically the first over the gunwales in a sea battle. Many sailors along the Middle Sea dive overboard rather than risk the scything steel of a Kyprion minotaur's axe.

LORE KEEPERS

A little information can be a dangerous thing. To guard against unwise, unwary, and unscrupulous knowledge seekers, a number of archives recruit minotaurs as trusty librarians. Not only do their size and strength dissuade common thieves, minotaurs can memorize dizzying library layouts and shelf organizations like no one else. Their recall of random facts can answer many peoples' casual questions. Their natural ferocity also lets them deal with any serious threats that appear, mundane or magical.

THINGS YOU MIGHT FIND ON A MINOTAUR…

Greataxe. Sailor's lantern. Salt-stained boiled leather armor. Tiny toy maze-cube. Supple leather and canvas clothing. Pair of hand axes. Staff carved with one of the following: book of riddles, the words carved in a spiral pattern; maze; pastoral country scenes; interlocking cog design; wise sayings; abstract designs. Large book. Heavy waterproofed sailors' cloak. Baling hook. Metal breastplate. Pouches containing coins (3d20 gp). Sack with a day's worth of food and spare clothes. Pouch containing bandages, hoof/horn glue, and a file. Sturdy knife. Leather gauntlets. Telescope. Whetstone and oil. Dagger from Triolo, the handle shaped like a fish-tail. Shaving kit. Ball of string.

MAGIC ITEMS

Imbroglio Axe (any axe). The maze etched upon the axe draws the eyes. *Once per battle:* The next enemy you hit becomes entranced by the patterns on your axe. For the rest of the battle when they move you may choose to move as a free action, provided it is to re-engage with them.
Quirk: Stubborn as a bull.

Staff of Dread Lore (staff - weapon/implement). The staff is made of sliding puzzle pieces that shift in combat. As a free action you can change the result of one damage die rolled (yours, an ally's, or an enemy's) to a different result, at the cost of expanding your fumble range by 1 for the rest of the battle.
Quirk: Obsessed with solving puzzles.

ADVENTURE HOOKS

The Red Chariot: Pirates have been plaguing shipping, so much so that every captain that can afford to do so has started hiring minotaur mercenaries. The captain of the Red Chariot cannot afford the suddenly high price for a full complement of mercenaries, so she pays the adventurers to round out the numbers. The first night out of port the adventurers overhear the minotaur mercenaries plotting. Are they in league with the pirates? Or are they arranging an "accident" to befall the party for undercutting their rates?

The Bull's 12 Labors: A minotaur begs the adventurers to escort her to a minotaur city where she hopes to have a curse removed. She claims to really be a kobold from Nuria Natal, whose alchemical experimentations led to her accidentally changing race. If the adventurers accompany her and keep her safe, she will reward them by being their personal alchemist. Is her story true? If so, how will the minotaurs react to it?

Kyprion Deckclearer

Better to jump into the briny deep than face a minotaur at sea...

Level 3 troop [HUMANOID]
Initiative: +14

Greataxe +8 vs. AC—10 damage

R: Hand axe +8 vs. AC
—5 damage
Natural odd miss: The minotaur may, as a quick action this round, pop free and move into engagement with a nearby enemy and make a *greataxe* attack at the end of that move.

Ship jumper: The deckclearer can leap from far away to engaged (or vice versa) with a single move action. This move does not draw an attack of opportunity.
Limited use: Twice per battle only.

AC 19
PD 17   **HP 45**
MD 14

Minotaur Librarian

Knowledge is power, but a swift and sturdy staff can be potent too.

Level 3 troop [HUMANOID]
Initiative: +14

Carved staff +8 vs. AC—10 damage
Natural even hit or miss: This turn the librarian may make a second *sturdy staff* attack as a quick action or may move as a quick action. Until the end of its next turn the librarian gains +2 to defenses against attacks that it provokes by moving.

Read the enemy: The librarian recognizes one enemy's fighting style, and only takes half damage from attacks made by that enemy.
Limited use: Once per battle only.

Random recall: The librarian gets a +5 bonus on checks to know a useful fact about history, geography, mathematics, geology, or zoology.

Stubborn: The librarian rolls 2x d20 for saves, and takes the best roll.

AC 19
PD 14   **HP 45**
MD 17

Minotaur Bodyguard

The minotaur guards' polished, rune-inscribed horns reflect the torchlight and tell their life stories. Both bear the First Blood rune, testifying to their skill.

Level 4 troop [HUMANOID]
Initiative: +15

Greataxe +6 vs. AC—14 damage (+8 damage if the target is engaged with the minotaur's protectee)

Protective presence: Once per battle as a free action the minotaur designates an ally as its protectee. Enemies nearby to the minotaur take a -2 penalty to attack rolls against the protectee.

[Special trigger] Protective charge: When a nearby enemy targets the minotaur's protectee with an attack, as a free action the minotaur pops free and moves to engage the attacker. The minotaur becomes the target of the attack, gaining a +2 bonus to defenses against the attack.
Limited use: Twice per battle only.

AC 20
PD 19   **HP 65**
MD 31

OWL HARPY

Living in abandoned buildings or cemeteries in the desert lands of the south, owl harpies are cousins to the more common harpies found in cooler climes. These elegant fliers glide silently through the night skies to patrol their territories and hunt for food—they eat any meat but favor desert rats and dogs. Owl harpies use their bittersweet songs to captivate intelligent prey before swooping down and tearing them into pieces with razor-sharp talons. Like owls, they can turn their heads nearly 360 degrees, making it very hard to catch one unawares.

STORYTELLERS AND SAGES

Scholars and adventurers from Siwal and other desert towns sometimes seek out owl harpies to question them about lost lore and ancient civilizations. Wise and knowledgeable, owl harpies have a great storytelling tradition that passes tales of history and legend from mother to daughter. Anyone wishing to learn secrets from an owl harpy storyteller should bring both fresh meat and shiny treasures to win her over.

THINGS YOU MIGHT FIND ON AN OWL HARPY...

Flute carved from a bone. Bag of candied mice. A book of just over one thousand short stories, most of which resemble commonly known stories but with surprising twists - the book itself is magical in a very minor way in that it contains more pages than its size would seem to suggest. Seventeen colored silk scarves. A sash trimmed with coins or bells. A silver charm bracelet. A veil.

MAGIC ITEMS

Veil of the Desert Moon (veil/head). A veil of shimmering material. *Recharge 16+:* As a quick action grant yourself +2 to all attacks that target MD for the rest of the battle.

Recharge 11+: For the next hour add +2 to all attempts to entice or beguile others.

Quirk: Hunger for live mice, scorpions, serpents, and other tiny desert creatures.

The 101 Never-Ending Tales (tome/implement). An enchanted storybook, there are always a couple of blank pages left for the current owner to fill with their own story. *Recharge 16+:* Cast *charm person* as a wizard or bard of your level.

Once per day: Add +2 to a knowledge style skill roll.

Quirk: Obsessively collect tales and add them to the book.

Dancer's Sash (belt). A length of multi-colored cloth hung with tiny bells. *Always:* Increase your maximum recoveries: +1 (adventurer); +2 (champion); +3 (epic). *Recharge 16+:* The first time in combat that you are missed by an attack gain temporary hit points equal to 5 x your level.

Recharge 16+: If not in battle you may dance, entrancing 1d6 enemies of your level or below with memories of your gyrating form. Entranced enemies start their next battle weakened and stuck (save ends). *Quirk:* Adorn yourself with bells and other music-making jewelry.

ADVENTURE HOOKS

Song of Sorrows: An owl harpy has found a song that will open up a demi-shadow road or semi-ley line and draw people onto it. She has used this song to travel, and to bring victims from all over Midgard to her hidden valley in the Dragoncoil mountains. The adventurers are just the latest in a long line of victims. If the adventurers are clever they might be able to learn the song—but it only works to bring them to this one valley. Why is this valley so special, and how did she learn the song?

The Scorpion's Tale: A cunning and accomplished storyteller travels all over Midgard spinning tales. That she is an owl harpy is obvious, but what is not known to those that she entertains and educates is that she is a spy for the Sultana. She has been carefully making maps, taking note of defenses, and building up a dossier on almost everybody of note or use that she meets. Now it is time for her to return and she has loaded up a wagon with her trunks full of notes. Unfortunately her wagon and mule are almost identical to that of the adventurers—causing some confusion among both her allies and enemies.

Owl Harpy

She flies on the velvet wings of night, and she's hungry for a feast...

Double strength level 5 blocker [HUMANOID]
Initiative: +12

Claw +10 vs. AC—14 damage
Natural even hit: 8 psychic damage and the harpy can make its *melancholy song* attack as a quick action this turn.

R: Shortbow +10 vs. AC—15 damage
Limited use: Not usable while flying.

C: Melancholy song +11 vs. MD (1d3 nearby enemies)—The target is drawn close to the owl harpy—though not engaged—and is stuck (save ends). Deafened creatures and other owl harpies are immune.

Swooping claws: On rounds where the escalation die is odd, the harpy may fly as a quick action instead of (or in addition to) a move action.

All-round vision: The harpy is hard to surprise. It never counts as being engaged with an ally of an enemy for purposes of attacks (such as *sneak attack*).

Exploits the captivated: The harpy deals +6 extra damage against stuck enemies.

I am death, a winged beast: The harpy can fly, swiftly and silently. The harpy can't hover, but it is very fast. When flying the owl harpy's movement doesn't provoke attacks.

AC 21
PD 17   **HP 72**
MD 18

Owl Harpy Storyteller

An owl-like woman perches on the roof ahead of you. She sings a mournful song that tells of a lonely fisherman who falls in love with a mermaid and drowns when he swims down to embrace her. Something about the melody draws you in.

Level 6 caster [HUMANOID]
Initiative: +14

Claw +11 vs. AC—32 damage
Natural even hit: 10 psychic damage and the harpy can make its *melancholy song* attack as a quick action this turn.

R: Thunderous proclamation +11 vs. PD—30 damage
Natural 16+ hit or miss: Target is stunned.

R: Terrifying fury +11 vs. PD—20 ongoing damage and the target is dazed (save ends both)
Once target saves: Target is dazed (save ends).
Limited use: May be used on rounds when the escalation die is odd only.

C: Melancholy song +11 vs. MD (1d3 nearby enemies)— The target is drawn close to the owl harpy—though not engaged—and is stuck (save ends). Deafened creatures and other owl harpies are immune.

Quatrain of recovery: As a quick action the owl harpy or a nearby ally ends all effects on them, pops free, and heals 30 hit points.
Limited use: Twice per battle only.

All-round vision: The harpy is hard to surprise. It never counts as being engaged with an ally of an enemy for purposes of attacks (such as *sneak attack*).

Exploits the captivated: The harpy deals +6 extra damage against stuck enemies.

I am death, a winged beast: The harpy can fly, swiftly and silently. The harpy can't hover, but it is very fast. When flying the owl harpy's movement doesn't provoke attacks.

AC 22
PD 18   **HP 180**
MD 19

ROACHLINGS

Roachlings, or scuttlers, appear throughout the world, especially in cramped, filthy locations that other races reject. Among the filth and debris of a city's dark alleys and slums, the roachlings scurrying forth in search of food and hidden treasure. Roachlings have a roughly humanoid shape with insectile features that include whip-like antennae in place of ears, a carapace that covers much of the back, small spines on their legs, and skin that appears oily but feels dry to the touch. They have no visible nose, and they have mandibles on either side of their mouths. Females are slightly larger but have smaller mandibles. Like the common cockroach, roachlings have wings but are rarely capable of serious flight. Most stand three to five feet tall, reach physical maturity at the age of 12, and can live as long as 80 years.

WILL TO SURVIVE

Though skittish and easily frightened, roachlings are not cowards, but they are practical. They understand survival sometimes means remaining unseen and out of reach. As a result, most roachlings prefer to attack only when the chance for victory sits squarely on their side.

When forced to fight, they attack with suicidal fury. Roachlings band together in tight groups and try to fight as one clicking mob. Those with warrior training often fight on after receiving mortal wounds.

DESPERATE DEMONS

The origins of the roachlings are shrouded in mystery. Some scholars believe that they were an agrarian race that did not resemble insects until they were uprooted by war and left to die as refugees in the bowels of a strange land. There, they found the one creature who would answer their prayers, Akyishigal the Skittish One, who offered them survival in exchange for being reshaped in his image.

Of all the dreadful demons lurking within the Abyss, perhaps none is as vile and disgusting as Akyishigal, the Skittish One, whose filth-slicked mandibles clack hungrily and ceaselessly for mortal flesh and souls. Despite this, he has a surprising number of followers among the urban dispossessed, the slum dwelling downtrodden, and those who lurk within the lightless depths beneath cities.

THINGS YOU MIGHT FIND ON A ROACHLING...

Ragged clothing. Length of pipe (used as a club). Tarnished knife, very sharp. Intricately worked leather vambraces of unsurpassed alien beauty. Throwing spikes. Cheap rusty caltrops. Bag of coins (filthy, but it is still money) 2d12 gp in coppers. Map of sewers, crawl-spaces, and narrow gaps between buildings. Rope, repaired and re-braided. Small cloth doll worn in a bag around the neck. Bag of rotted fruit, moldy bread, and scraps of fresh meat. Broken string of pearls (worth 3d6 gp). Slightly tarnished diamond ring (worth d20x50 gp). Symbol of Akyishigal.

MAGIC ITEMS

Roachlings don't usually make magic items, nor can they be made into magic items. However, roachlings can scrounge up the most unlikely things. Pick a magic item from elsewhere and give it a flaw:

Temperamental: It can only activate special abilities while the escalation die is odd ('always' abilities work fine).

Backfires: After a special ability is used roll a d10 for what condition you suffer (1= Dazed. 2= Hampered. 3= Stuck. 4= Stunned. 5= Vulnerable. 6= Weakened. 7-10= No effect). Save ends the condition.

Broken: Odd special effects when the item is in use, different each time. When you roll initiative the GM tells you the effect: your hair and clothes might turn blue, or you might shrink an inch, or your voice might become squeaky, or you might grow an extra face, or you might teleport 1" every time you sneeze. Generally the strangeness wears off after a couple of hours.

ADVENTURE HOOKS

The Metamorphosis: A human priest offers to bless the party before they set off for their latest adventure. All characters who agree to be blessed gain +2 to all rolls, but upon completing the quest they discover that they are slowly turning into roachlings. They need to find the priest and have him undo whatever he has done, but the locals says that he turned into a roachling one morning and headed into the sewers. The adventurers must travel among the downtrodden and destitute to find the priest of He Who Scuttles.

Greasepaint and Black Cloth: A new theatre called the Emerald Butterfly has opened in town, making clever use of roachlings as puppeteers and stage hands. Wearing all black clothing they can move about the stage almost unseen, able to create startlingly good effects simply by moving bits of colored cloth or holding aloft painted wood. The roachlings, however, are finding that not everybody feels that the show must go on. A troupe of illusionists wants the Emerald Butterfly shutdown, and threats have been made. The Roachlings wish to hire the adventurers as protection, but the illusionists have a counter-offer.

Roachling Urban Scuttler

It shies away from the light as though frightened. But then you hear the scuttling sounds from the shadows and realize it's not alone.

Level 5 mook [HUMANOID]
Initiative: +10

Dagger +10 vs. AC—9 damage

Four armed warrior: If the roachling rolls a 2, 3, or 4 when making a weapon attack roll, it rerolls and takes the second roll.

Pustulent innards: When the roachling dies all nearby creatures that are not roachlings take 6 poison damage.

Tenacious survivor: Once per battle when the roachling would be reduced to 0 hit points, it is instead reduced to 5 hit points and becomes dazed until the end of the battle.

Flight: The roachling can unfurl insectile wings and fly. It is a heavy, clumsy flier that cannot get more than a couple of feet off the ground, though if it launches from a height it can maintain altitude for about five minutes before it has to land. Buzzing wings and rattling wing-cases make stealthy flying impossible. Roachlings never take falling damage.

Resist poison 16+: When a poison attack targets this creature, the attacker must roll a natural 16+ on the attack roll or it only deals half damage.

AC 21
PD 20   **HP 18 (mook)**
MD 17

Mook: Kill one roachling urban scuttler mook for every 18 damage you deal to the mob.

Roachling Servant

They do the jobs that others won't, and are poorly paid for it.

Level 6 mook [HUMANOID]
Initiative: +14

Biting mass +11 vs. AC—12 damage
Natural 16+ hit or miss: Target becomes vulnerable to all roachling attacks (save ends).

Four armed warrior: If the roachling rolls a 2, 3, or 4 when making a weapon attack roll, it rerolls and takes the second roll.

Pustulent innards: When the roachling dies all nearby creatures that are not roachlings take 6 poison damage.

Swarm attack: Enemies who end their turn engaged with the roachling take 5 damage.

Tenacious survivor: Once per battle when the roachling would be reduced to 0 hit points it instead becomes dazed until the end of the battle.

Flight: The roachling can unfurl insectile wings and fly. It is a heavy, clumsy flier that cannot get more than a couple of feet off the ground, though if it launches from a height it can maintain altitude for about five minutes before it has to land. Buzzing wings and rattling wing-cases make stealthy flying impossible. Roachlings never take falling damage.

Resist poison 16+: When a poison attack targets this creature, the attacker must roll a natural 16+ on the attack roll or it only deals half damage.

AC 22
PD 21   **HP 23 (mook)**
MD 18

Mook: Kill one roachling servant mook for every 23 damage you deal to the mob.

Roachling Warrior

You always thought "roachling warrior" was an oxymoron. Then you faced one in combat, wielding a short sword in each of its four clawed hands.

Level 7 mook [HUMANOID]
Initiative: +16

Filthy claw +12 vs. AC—18 damage
Natural 16+ hit or miss: Target becomes vulnerable to all roachling attacks (save ends).

Astonishing bladework +12 vs. AC—20 damage
Natural 16+ hit: The target is dazed and the roachling can make a second *astonishing bladework* attack as a quick action for 5 damage.

C: Fetid reek +12 vs. PD (1d3 nearby enemies) —9 poison damage and the target is hampered (save ends).
Limited use: On rounds where the escalation die is odd only.

Four armed warrior: If the roachling rolls a 2, 3, or 4 when making a weapon attack roll it rerolls and takes the second roll.

Pustulent innards: When the roachling dies all nearby creatures that are not roachlings take 6 poison damage.

Tenacious survivor: Once per battle when the roachling would be reduced to 0 hit points it instead becomes dazed until the end of the battle.

Flight: The roachling can unfurl insectile wings and fly. It is a heavy, clumsy flier that cannot get more than a couple of feet off the ground, though if it launches from a height it can maintain altitude for about five minutes before it has to land. Buzzing wings and rattling wing-cases make stealthy flying impossible. Roachlings never take falling damage.

Resist poison 16+: When a poison attack targets this creature, the attacker must roll a natural 16+ on the attack roll or it only deals half damage.

AC 23
PD 22   **HP 27 (mook)**
MD 19

Mook: Kill one roachling warrior mook for every 27 damage you deal to the mob.

ROTHENIAN CENTAUR

Centaurs are strange, half-human wanderers with no fixed home. On the Rothenian Plains, they are friends and rivals to the Windrunner elves, half-foolish and half-wise when moved by drink or rage. Centaurs live in small clans—sometimes numbering only a dozen or so—and all too often serve as mercenaries, fighting someone else's war for little more than meat and cheese. When roused to anger, they burn out entire villages and sack small towns before returning to the plains, richer and avenged.

NOMADIC HUNTERS

Out in the extensive grasslands far to the east of Zobeck and high in the hills, larger bands of fiercely independent centaurs live as hunters, bandits, and nomads. They serve only their chiefs and khans and would die rather than settle down. Those who do not understand the centaurs' nomadic ways fear their violent tempers and wild passions. Centaurs think settled creatures fools to huddle in huts of wood or stone when they could live free on the great grasslands. These horsefolk could not live any other way. The centaurs are true nomads, retreating to hills and Rothenian high meadows in summer and returning to lower elevations when the meadows are bare and the lure of rustling, banditry, and raiding grow strong.

Centaurs follow many gods, but Perun (god of lightning and war) and Porevit (in his aspect as god of wine and fertility) are most popular. These gods' penchants for violence, drink, and generally poor impulse control, appeals greatly to the centaurs' sense of wildness and the madness and freedom of their nomadic lives.

Centaurs have a long tradition of healing and medicine, derived from both herbal and divine sources. This medicine is mostly meant for horses and centaurs and is remarkable in its ability to save even abused horses from the brink of starvation, strangles, or spongy hoof.

In battle, centaurs use large steppe lances, often decorated with banners and tassels, and enormous recurved longbows made from wood, sinew, and horn. They can easily trample their foes underfoot but are also surprisingly skilled at stealth and wood-craft, making excellent scouts. Centaurs fear confined spaces and steep slopes; they cannot climb walls or cliffs, and narrow or spiral stairs are difficult. They rarely enter towns, preferring the open road. They are currently divided into those who live free in the eastern grasslands and those who hunt and serve as mercenaries in human lands.

IMPERIAL BODYGUARDS

Long ago, some centaurs turned their backs on the Rothenian Plains and made their homes in the lands of the Seven Cities. The centaurs of the Rhoetian Guard are the most feared section of the Valeran cavalry, forming the vanguard of the August Republic's mounted forces and acting as personal protectors to the young Emperor of Valera. While many of the centaur legionnaires are known as loutish brutes who take what they want from the citizens of Valera, the Rhoetians cling to an ancient honor code of personal service to the emperor.

There are a few Rhoetians who have abandoned the old ways, however, and found great success as mercenaries.

Larger than the most massive warhorse, the centaurs of the Rhoetian Guard are more than a match for the heavy cavalry of Valera's enemies. They begin battle by firing their heavy crossbows and then charging with lances fixed. Once in the thick of combat, Rhoetians lay about with heavy sabers and kick and trample their opponents with abandon.

THINGS YOU MIGHT FIND
ON A ROTHENIAN CENTAUR...

Centaur-sized recurved horn bow. Falchion. Tooled leather breastplate. Metal breastplate. Crested helm. Lance. Javelins. Ornate sword. Heavy crossbow. Tool for removing stones from hooves. Horseshoes. Throwing knives in hip scabbards. War banner. Plate barding. Bag containing loot (roll d10 2d4 times for the contents, and 3d20 for the gp worth of each item: 1= 3d6 Dented golden goblets. 2= Silver candlesticks. 3= Strings of pearls. 4= Pewter religious statues. 5= Tapestry. 6= Silks. 7= Broken gold statues. 8= Silver mirror. 9= Various jewels pried loose from their settings. 10-12= Coins.)

MAGIC ITEMS

The Nail That Wins Battles (boot/foot). An enchanted golden nail, made to keep a horseshoe on; but if stitched onto a boot it will be fooled into giving up its magic. The first time in a battle that you engage somebody, after you attack you can pop free and move.

Recharge 6+: You may run over water for a short distance—probably enough to cross a moat or small river. If you stop or slow down you sink.

Quirk: You could run faster if you were naked!

Lance of Glory (lance / heavy two-handed spear, melee). Many small starbursts are engraved down the length of the shaft. If this is your first round engaged with a non-mook enemy and you reduce it to 0 hit points with your first blow, you may pop free and move as a quick action.

Quirk: Shout victory cries at inopportune times.

ADVENTURE HOOKS

The Thunder of Distant Hooves: The Seven Cities have recently been plagued by centaur bandits, and the Valerans do not fully trust the Rhoetian Guard to catch the miscreants. The Valerians insist that outside observers, the adventurers, accompany the Rhoetian Guard. The adventurers now have the unenviable task of trying to keep up with resentful centaurs who are chasing other centaurs.

The Voice of Perun: A centaur claiming to be a holy prophet of Perun has been going around performing wondrous works. He claims that riding horses into battle is against the will of his god, for only centaurs may charge into battle on hooves. Ordinarily no one would pay attention, except that wherever he goes, a couple of days later horses start going wild: trying to escape, refusing to be ridden or even saddled. Even mules refuse to pull carts. Something needs to be done, but what?

Rothenian Centaur Bandit

Swifter than a human, more cunning than a horse. Centaurs are nomadic raiders who take what they want by force.

Level 2 troop [BEAST]
Initiative: +8

Lance and falchion +7 vs. AC—5 damage
Natural 16+ hit: +5 damage.
[Special] Charging centaur: If the centaur has just moved into engagement with the target, the centaur gains +2 to hit. If the target is hit it pops free of engagement after the attack.

R: Rothenian bow +7 vs. AC—7 damage
[Special] Pounding hooves: The centaur can make this attack mid-move.

Trample: If an enemy misses the centaur with an opportunity attack, the enemy takes 8 damage.

AC 18
PD 16   **HP 36**
MD 12

Rothenian Centaur Chief

A chief of the nomadic bandits, he can infuse his bow with magic to strike back at wizards and sorcerers.

Level 3 troop [BEAST]
Initiative: +9

Lance and falchion +8 vs. AC—8 damage
[Special] Charging centaur: If the centaur has just moved into engagement with the target, the centaur gains +2 to hit. If the target is hit it pops free of engagement after the attack.

R: Nomad's longbow +8 vs. AC—10 damage
Natural 16+ hit: Target is stuck (save ends).
[Special] Pounding hooves: The centaur can make this attack mid-move.

[Special trigger] Spellseeker: If the centaur is targeted by a spell it may immediately make a *nomad's longbow* attack against the caster as a free action. If the shot hits, the spell is not cast.

Trample: If an enemy misses the centaur with an opportunity attack, the enemy takes 8 damage.

AC 19
PD 17   **HP 45**
MD 13

Rothenian Centaur Roughneck

The centaur has shod its hooves in steel and uses them to smash foes as swings its sword.

Level 4 troop [BEAST]
Initiative: +10

Sabre and steel shod hooves +9 vs. AC—11 damage
Natural even hit: The target becomes vulnerable to melee attacks until its next turn.
Natural 16+ hit: +7 damage.

[Special] Charging centaur: If the centaur has just moved into engagement with the target, the centaur gains +2 to hit. If the target is hit it pops free of engagement after the attack.

R: Crossbow +8 vs. AC—13 damage

[Special] Pounding hooves: The centaur can make this attack mid-move.

Trample: If an enemy misses the centaur with an opportunity attack the enemy takes 8 damage.

AC 20
PD 18   **HP 54**
MD 14

SHADOW FEY

Called scáthsidhe (pronounced SCAH-shee) by other fey, or simply shadow fey by mortals, these dark faeries are counted among the Unseelie, though they resent it. They simply call themselves the sidhe and consider themselves an extension of the Seelie Court. To most, the shadow fey are little more than a dancing darkness among the leaves.

Shadow fey prefer to hold conversations with foes or strangers from hiding. When seen, they have long arms and wide grins in fair features, with skin tones varying from ash gray to brown. Their gray, black, or green eyes are unusually large, and their ears are pointed. Some have tiny horns hidden among their clouds of white or silver hair. Shadow fey usually carry a rapier or falchion made from exotic materials from their home plane, such as black silver.

TRICKSY FOES

Shadow fey generally remain concealed until confident of victory. They prefer weapons, spells, and minions that weaken and torment their enemies rather than kill quickly. They will kill mounts, sabotage equipment, and steal valuables before striking. Shadow fey prefer talking to entice others to join them in service to the Goddess of Night and Magic, since violence rarely produces converts.

Shadow fey build their cities and villages in the forests of the Plane of Shadow. They enjoy homes with sharp shadows or constantly flickering lights, conditions most other creatures find disconcerting or irksome.

Though most shadow fey live in communities, some lead solitary lives for reasons unknown to mortals. Whether exiles, scouts, lawbreakers, hermits, or something else, these loners are often strange, inscrutable, and dangerous even by scáthsidhe standards.

SHADOW DWELLERS

The scáthsidhe are powerful on their home plane and widely renowned for tainting other creatures with darkness or light and ensnaring them into the service of their goddess. Shadow fey have a complex society, serving the Moonlight King, the Queen of Shadows, and their bloodline called the Shadow House. Ultimately all shadow fey obey this structure, though its power is strongest in their cities and palace on the Plane of Shadow. They consider themselves the equals of the Seelie Court, though the Seelie do not acknowledge them as more than distant relatives.

The other noble houses of the shadow fey are transient but currently include the Flicker House, Dawn House, Lucent House, and Fading House, among others. The great nobles include the Black Prince, the Duke of Alabaster, the Twilight Duchess, and the Glimmering Prince. All of these nobles follow the Goddess of Night and Magic to varying degrees, although some just make a show of piety.

Shadow fey strictly avoid the use of personal names and choose natural elements and nicknames to avoid granting others too much power over them. Names such as Noon, Midnight, Shine, Glimmer, Gray, and Charcoal are very common. Others go by Raven, Dove, Fox, or similar animal names.

THINGS YOU MIGHT FIND ON A SHADOW FEY...

A rapier forged of black silver during an eclipse. A lyre, made of wood from a house fire and stringed with ghost-wails. A silken robe woven by a blind spider-witch. A hair pin, crafted out of coral grown on the tallest spire of a sunken castle. A silver compact containing face powder, the pearls on the compact are all from oysters that are really polymorphed widows. A beautiful belt, woven from shed naga skin and gnome tongues. A pouch of money that will fade as soon as it is handed to another. A magical comb which lengthens any hair it is run through by an inch per minute of combing. A magical needle: if put into loose cloth or clothing will summon forth animated ghostly scissors, needles, pins, etc. and will produce a formal gown or similar garment from the material.

MORE THINGS YOU MIGHT FIND ON A SHADOW FEY...

A length of slim silver chain (wondrous item, requires attunement, use 1/day) that when shaken at a door or similar casts *hold portal* as though it were a 5th level wizard. A hand-mirror (wondrous item, requires attunement, use 1/day) that can cast *disguise self* at the owner's command as though it were a 5th level wizard. A feather brooch (wondrous item, requires attunement, use 1/day) that can cast *feather-fall* or *levitate* at the owner's command as though it were a 5th level wizard. Cosmetics (wondrous item, requires attunement, use 1/day) that when applied to the lips allows the wearer to cast *message* or *speak with item* as though they were a 5th level wizard. A dagger forged from uncomfortable truths, with the hilt made of comforting lies (looks like glass, acts like steel, apart from that is not magical, grants no bonus, and does not require attunement).

MAGIC ITEMS

Moxxien Gem (wondrous item) These decorative gems empower well-crafted weapons and armor when attached:

Weapon: +1 to hit and damage (adventurer); +2 (champion); +3 (epic).

Armor: +1 AC (adventurer); +2 AC (champion); +3 AC (epic).

Helmet or circlet: +1 MD (adventurer); +2 MD (champion); +3 MD (epic).

Note: These bonuses do not stack with existing bonuses from a magic item nor with each other. For example, adding multiple epic gems to epic armor only gets you +3 AC, though each of the gems and the armor would still benefit you through their additional abilities.

Special: Each type of gem has a different effect (see below).

Quirk: Vain and cruel.

Hawk's Eye Quartz Once per day when targeted by a ranged attack roll a save. On a success the attacker becomes the target of their own attack instead of you.

Green Onyx Once per day for one battle, while you are engaged with a creature that has a fear aura, you regain hit points equal to the escalation die value at the start of each of your turns.

Fire Opal You are immune to normal fires, your unarmed attacks do fire damage, and you have resist fire 11+.

Blood Jade Once per day when a nearby creature heals, you may spend a recovery to heal as a free action.

Moon Pearl Once per day choose a creature type (humanoid, undead, construct, etc.). For the rest of the day you are aware of the exact location of any nearby creatures of that type. Effects such as *blur* or *invisibility* do not affect your ability to target them.

ADVENTURE HOOKS

The Payment: A shadow fey emissary approaches the party to pay them for their memories. *"Oh no,"* she explains, *"I don't want more memories. You've already traded some memories, here is your payment"*. The party can't remember trading away their memories for bags of powdered silver that hangs in the air with the sound of innocent laughter—but apparently they have. When they check on the date it is a month later than they were expecting, their boots are muddy, their armor has new dents. Something happened in that month and they chose to sell their memories of it. Will the party try to find out what it is they can't remember? Or will they decide that they must have sold their memories for a reason, and hope that what they can't remember will not cause complications?

Shadow Fey Courtier

The fair man resembles an elf, but something in his cloying smile and hooded eyes hints at sharpened teeth and dark intents.

Level 5 troop [HUMANOID]
Initiative: +13

Darting rapier +10 vs. AC—18 damage

Natural odd hit or miss: The next time the fey uses *flickering shroud* this battle it uses it as a quick action instead of a standard action.

Flickering shroud: As a standard action the shadow fey becomes shrouded from sight and teleports to any point nearby or far away. It is a DC 25 check to spot the shadow fey while it is shrouded (enemies only know approximately where it is). If an enemy has not spotted the shadow fey, the enemy takes a -4 penalty to hit the shadow fey and is vulnerable to attacks made by the shadow fey. After the shadow fey next attacks its shroud ends.

Bloody reversal: When an enemy misses the shadow fey with a melee attack the shadow fey may immediately use its *flickering shroud* ability. If it moves so that it is engaged with the attacker that triggered the ability, and the escalation die is odd, it may make an immediate *darting rapier* attack.

Sharp eyes: The shadow fey can see perfectly well in even very low light conditions, but not in total darkness. Provided there is a candle or starlight, the shadow fey can see as clear as though it were a bright day.

AC 21
PD 19   **HP 72**
MD 15

Shadow Fey Rake

The shadow fey is cool, calm, totally in control. It holds its stance for three heartbeats and then lunges...

Level 6 troop [HUMANOID]
Initiative: +11

Dashing rapier +11 vs. AC—21 damage

Natural 16+ hit or miss: The rake pops free.

Skilled parry: Once per round when an enemy misses the shadow fey with a melee attack, the shadow fey may immediately make a *dashing rapier* attack against that enemy as a free action.

Duelists poise: The shadow fey rake gains +2 to hit with opportunity attacks and gains +2 to defenses against opportunity attacks.

Sharp eyes: The shadow fey can see perfectly well in even very low light conditions, but not in total darkness. Provided there is a candle or starlight on a clear night, the shadow fey can see as clear as though it were a bright day.

AC 22
PD 16   **HP 90**
MD 20

Shadow Fey Shadowsworn

The scent of lost dreams lingers around the shadow fey. Your mind wanders, musing on past regrets. You fail to notice the patterns it draws in the air.

Level 7 caster [HUMANOID]
Initiative: +12

R: Shadow owl talons +12 vs. MD—28 psychic damage and the target is teleported to a spot nearby, and is vulnerable to all attacks until the start of its next turn

Natural 14+ miss: Target pops free, is pushed slightly away from the fey, and is hampered (easy save ends).

Natural 16+ hit or miss: An additional (second) nearby enemy pops free, is pushed slightly away from the fey, and is hampered (save ends).

Natural 18+ hit or miss: An additional (third) nearby enemy pops free, is pushed slightly away from the fey, and is hampered (hard save ends).

R: Unravel +12 vs. MD—Choose one effect on the target, or which is produced or controlled by the target; such as a summoned creature, an wizard's ongoing spell effect, a bard's song, a paladin's challenge, a rogue's momentum, a monk's position in a form, a barbarian's rage, a bonus to attack rolls or defenses, flying, etc. The effect ends. If used on an ally, *unravel* automatically hits.

Miss: The next time *shadow owl talons* is used it does not provoke attacks if cast in melee.

Flickering shroud: As a standard action the shadow fey becomes shrouded from sight and teleports to any point nearby or far away. It is a DC 25 check to spot the shadow fey while it is shrouded (enemies only know approximately where it is). If an enemy has not spotted the shadow fey, the enemy takes a -4 penalty to hit the shadow fey and is vulnerable to attacks made by the shadow fey. After the shadow fey next attacks its shroud ends.

Summoned shadows: For this battle the battlefield is illuminated only by dim light, even on a bright day. The effect ends when the shadowsworn dies.

Sharp eyes: The shadow fey can see perfectly well in even very low light conditions, but not in total darkness. Provided there is a candle or starlight on a clear night, the shadow fey can see as clear as though it were a bright day.

Alternate form: As a quick action the shadow fey shadowsworn may transform into a small white, black, or gray animal such as a raven, dove, cat, owl, or fox. The shadow fey shadowsworn cannot use powers in this form. Transforming back is a move action.

AC 23
PD 21   **HP 108**
MD 17

ZOBECK GEARFORGED

As the children of Rava—the Gear Goddess of fate and industry—gearforged are mechanical wonders that each house the soul of a once-living mortal. Rava's priests first worked with craftsmen and mages to forge bodies and cunning mechanisms of brass, copper, and steel in support of Zobeck's Great Revolt. A special ritual transfers a living creature's soul into the housing, and this separates the gearforged from mere clockwork. A gearforged can, in theory, live forever, though in practice most wind down or are destroyed by the ravages of time.

METAL BUT MORTAL

Without exception, gearforged are shaped as humanoids, and the vast majority of those are one of two styles: roughly human-sized, with articulated joints, hands, feet, and magical eyes; or a rather stouter version made by the dwarves, sometimes called geardwarves. These dwarf-like gearforged are more common in the cantons of the Ironcrags than in Zobeck, but several do labor ceaselessly in the Gear District. In the south, minotaur gearforged are rare but not entirely unknown. Nicknamed Ironhorns, they act as elite enforcers and guards.

A very few gearforged are built to smaller sizes, believed to be intended for kobold souls, but these are subject to frequent failure and even the extinction of the souls they carry. And that is, of course, the core fact of all gearforged: they were once something quite variable, adaptable, and alive. Now they are a somewhat standardized collection of cylinders, springs, and articulated joints of varying quality.

INTELLIGENT CONSTRUCTS

The gearforged are thinking creatures and serve the city as watchmen, members of the Spyglass Guild, and soldiers. Each is a unique individual, as distinctive in appearance as any other people, though their basic framework is always humanoid. Unlike clockwork creatures, which are merely servants responsive to orders and capable of little more than a limited amount of memorization, gearforged have free will.

Their mechanisms are more than mechanical, of course, because all gearforged have a soul. Their limbs use actuators powered by everwound springs. Their minds depend on memory gears, transverse cognition gearing, and the marvel of a soul gem connected directly to a maze of silver and mithral steam, spark, and magical conduits. These elements are all held in a shell of iron, brass, and steel, and the bulk of the thing is quite remarkable. A large and heavily armored gearforged can weigh 400 pounds, as its armor is often built in.

UNDYING LEGION, BIRTHED IN BATTLE

The gearforged were mortal, once. When the Collegium sided with the rebels against House Stross during the Great Revolt, the Steamworkers and Geargrinders built gearforged bodies as fast as the forges allowed, and the priests of Rava and clockwork mages animated more than 100 mechanical knights to counter the nobles' heavy cavalry. The required spirits came from the people of the city: elderly volunteers, angry and idealistic young men, criminals seeking a reprieve, and a few broken individuals seeking a new life in a whole body. Their bodies died, but their souls lived, and fought, and won.

Since then, a few souls join the first gearforged every year. Many are wealthy merchants at the end of life, others soldiers seeking a new edge, and a few are criminals compelled to serve the city as the price of their crimes. Many of the first clockwork legionnaires who stood against House Stross still defend the Free City. They command and lead the growing gearforged core of Zobeck's army, which is respected throughout the Crossroads and the Seven Cities.

THINGS YOU MIGHT FIND ON A GEARFORGED...

Icon of Rava. Set of folding gearwork tools. A cloth and a small bottle of oil. A memento of a former life (Roll d8: 1= Locket with a picture of a child in it. 2= Lock of braided hair. 3= A stone worn on a string (looks like a bit of masonry). 4= A cloth doll. 5= A leather bracelet. 6= A ring, worth d100gp. 6= A watch. 7= A tin medallion. 8= A diary.)

MAGIC ITEMS

Cogwork weapon (any weapon). The intricate meshing cogs whir and blur into action when the weapon is in use. When you roll a critical hit with this weapon your crit range expands by 2 for the rest of the battle.

Quirk: Constantly tinkering with things.

Blessed Cogs of Rava (wondrous item). The leather bag never quite seems to run out of cogs. Each day this bag regenerates 1d3 cogs (to a maximum of 6). Expend a cog by throwing it at a solid surface. The cog will whir and multiply for several minutes before merging with the surface and producing one of the following (depending on the will of the user):

1. A locked door with a key, the door is attached to a doorway through a wall (or into a cupboard if there is no void on the other side of the wall for the door to open into) and is made of interlocking cogs.
2. A two-story brass spiral staircase made of cogs.
3. A small 10x10x10' room or a 20x5x5' corridor or shaft. The new room will generally feature cogs and pipes and maybe machinery of no definite purpose.
4. A 10x10x10 wall of interlocking cogs (or a 20x10x5 wall or a 40x5x5 wall).

Note that the cogs do not create extra-dimensional spaces, they merely excavate and construct using available materials.

Quirk: Trespass for knowledge, build for victory.

Spark Blade (any sword, spear, or staff). The twin pronged blade crackles with energy. Attacks with this weapon that have no damage type instead do lightning damage.

Once Per Day: Touch the weapon to a pile of junk and it transforms into a small mechanical creature. Use the rules for a wizard's familiar for this creature; the GM decides upon its specific abilities. It will serve you as a familiar for one day and will then leave your service.

Quirk: You hate to throw anything away.

Symbol of Perfect Mending (holy symbol). This holy symbol of Rava ticks, though no mechanism can be seen. Gain a bonus to hit and damage with cleric spells, or with wizard spells if you are a specialist gear mage or are a wizard with a background relating to fixing mechanisms +1 (adventurer); +2 (champion); +3 (epic).

Recharge 11+: You may do one of the following:
1. Cast the *mend* spell, summoning forth tiny cog-sprites.
2. Spend a recovery to recharge a magic item with a recharge ability.
3. You or a nearby ally may regain hit points as though you had spent a recovery, provided one of you has an item with a recharge ability that may still be used. That item then counts as having used that ability and failed to recharge it.

Quirk: Precise, like clockwork.

ADVENTURE HOOKS

Divine Echoes: A secretive cult of heretical gearforged are donating memory gears to a machine they are building. They hope that this machine will achieve apotheosis and become a god. For now they are interested in obtaining parts and remaining hidden. Surprisingly it appears that their god is real—or at least might one day become real—and the power of that god is echoing backward through time. The voice of the yet-to-be-constructed god has named the party as saints. Do the adventurers accept their role as saints of an unbirthed machine god, or do they work to bring down the cult? What will followers of Rava think of this, if and when they find out?

Zobeck Legionnaire

Clearly a mechanical construct, the creature resembles a humanoid woman with a huge sword and a strangely incongruous braid of chestnut hair. It regards you with metal eyes that shine with intelligence.

Level 3 troop [CONSTRUCT]
Initiative: +5

Bastard sword and shield +8 vs. AC—10 damage
Natural even hit: The legionnaire bashes the target with its shield and the target pops free.

R: Clockwork crossbow +8 vs. AC—10 damage

Clockwork resilience: All saving throws against ongoing damage are an easy save.

AC 22
PD 17   **HP 32**
MD 13

Geardwarf Marksman

Perfect soldiers, these living constructs feel no pain and have little fear of death. They've already died once.

Level 3 archer [CONSTRUCT]
Initiative: +5

Slam +8 vs. AC—10 damage. *Slam* does 20 damage if the geardwarf has less than 23 hit points)

R: Hand cannon +8 vs. PD—10 fire damage
Limited use: The geardwarf cannot use *hand cannon* if it has less than 23 hit points.

Cannon combustion: When the geardwarf drops to less than 23 hit points it immediately makes this attack:
[Special trigger] **C: Cannon combustion +10 vs. PD (1d3 nearby enemies, usually those closest to the construct)**—10 fire damage and 5 ongoing fire damage (save ends)
Limited use: If the geardwarf's hit points rises to 23 hit points or above it regains the use of this attack for the next time it drops below the hit points threshold.

Clockwork resilience: All saving throws against ongoing damage are an easy save.

AC 19
PD 17   **HP 45**
MD 13

Gearforged Assassin

As accurate as a watch, as implacable as death itself. The gearforged assassin's metal body is enchanted with magic that lets it blend in like a chameleon with any environment.

Level 4 troop [CONSTRUCT]
Initiative: +6

Kukri +12 vs. AC—14 damage
Natural even hit or miss: Gain a use of *camouflage*.

Camouflage: The assassin may make a move action that does not provoke attacks and becomes hidden (DC 20 to spot) until it attacks. If the assassin starts its turn hidden it gains +2 to hit on its first attack that turn.
Limited use: The assassin starts each battle with only one use of *camouflage*. Every time it rolls a natural even attack roll (hit or miss) it gains another use of the ability.

Assassin's strike: When the assassin makes an attack against an enemy that is engaged with an ally of the assassin, the assassin deals an extra 4 points of damage on a hit or miss.

Clockwork resilience: All saving throws against ongoing damage are an easy save.

AC 20
PD 18
MD 13   **HP 40**

Saint of Rava

The most fanatical of Rava's gearforged followers—and some are truly zealots—are called the saints. They are generally implanted with a third hand and a third eye, said to be Rava's Hand and Rava's Eyes in the world. Indeed, sometimes the goddess does seem to see through the eye and react, writing instructions to her saints or prophesying through the Clockwork Oracle, based on those distant eyes. In some sense, the saints are her distant and distributed minds and hands.

Level 4 leader [CONSTRUCT]
Initiative: +7

Scimitar +9 vs. AC—14 damage

R: Furnace strike +8 vs. PD—7 holy damage and 5 ongoing fire damage.

Blessings of Rava: The saint can communicate with all machines and constructs. Three times per battle the saint may either (a) move a single construct ally up one place in the initiative order, or (b) grant a reroll to a construct ally who missed with an attack.

Blessed mending: Each round the saint can restore 5 hit points to itself or a nearby construct ally, or restore 3 hit points to a nearby non-construct ally.

Clockwork resilience: All saving throws against ongoing damage are an easy save.

AC 20
PD 18
MD 14   **HP 54**

Gearforged Ironhorn

A hulking gearforged minotaur snorting fire and steam? Better bring reinforcements.

Double strength level 6 troop [CONSTRUCT]
Initiative: +10

Greataxe +14 vs. AC—42 damage

Iron gore +14 vs. AC—52 damage and 10 ongoing damage from bleeding (save ends)
Limited use: Once per battle immediately following a move action to engage

C: Ringing hoof stomp +14 vs. PD (1d3 nearby enemies)—32 thunder damage and the target pops free

Clockwork resilience: All saving throws against ongoing damage are an easy save.

AC 19
PD 17   **HP 180**
MD 13

Player Character Races

Centaurs

+2 Dexterity OR +2 Constitution

These half-human, half-horse nomads are known for their healing arts, skill with bow and sword, and poor impulse control. Centaurs don't have much time for reading or for learning magic. Those that do sometimes wind up as adventurers.

HARNESSED SPEED (RACIAL POWER)

You gain a +4 AC bonus against opportunity attacks.

Champion Feat: When an enemy makes an opportunity attack against you and misses, you immediately deal 10 damage to that enemy.

Epic Feat: When an enemy makes an opportunity attack against you and hits or misses, you immediately deal 10 damage to that enemy.

Darakhul

+2 Charisma, No Constitution: Use your Charisma score in place of your Constitution score when calculating hit points, AC, PD, Constitution-related checks, and any talent or other ability that relies on Constitution. When generating a darakhul character using a point buy system, you must still spend sufficient points for a Constitution score of 10.

They call themselves the People, but the rest of Midgard calls them the Lords Subterranean, the Ghoul Imperium, or simply the Empire of the Ghouls. Their cities lie out of sight, their agents infiltrate the underworlds of a score of surface cities, and their goals know no limits. To them, if you are not a member of the People, you are food. They are the darakhul.

By definition, both ordinary ghouls and darakhul arise from the infected and fallen of other races, but darakhul PCs start play as lesser darakhul. Any bonuses, penalties, and abilities of the previous race are gone; only their cosmetic features remain. Over time these pointed ears, long beards, or similar features fade into the bald, fanged features and pale, grey skin of the ghoul races.

Playing as an undead creature that constantly hungers for living flesh presents some…complexities. We don't recommend it for inexperienced players, or for groups where not everyone's completely comfortable with having a ghoul in the party. You can find more ideas for playing a darakhul in **Advanced Races: Darakhul.**

GHOUL OF THE IMPERIUM (RACIAL POWER)

Being a ghoul has its benefits—and its disadvantages.

Undead: You do not breathe, eat, or sleep or get tired. You are immune to ongoing poison damage, and to the confused, dazed, fear, stunned, and weakened effects. Negative energy damage heals you instead. Healing spells and potions do not affect you. You are vulnerable to holy attacks, and are affected by spells, attacks, abilities, talents and powers that target undead. If you are reduced to 0 hit points or less you are immediately destroyed (no death saves). You cannot

be returned to life/undeath by anything that raises or reincarnates the dead. *Resurrection* returns you to life as your original race—not as a darakhul.

Darkvision: You can see in the dark as well as a normal human can in full daylight.

Daylight weakness: You suffer a -4 penalty to attacks, skill and ability checks when in full daylight.

Champion Feat: With practice, you've learned to better handle the effects of the sun. You reduce the penalty from being in the sunlight from -4 to -2.

Hunger for flesh: You are always hungry—hunger defines your very existence. When you are around living creatures it takes iron discipline to keep from killing and eating them. To heal during a quick rest, you must consume a small meal of raw meat. To take a full heal-up, you must spend one hour consuming an amount of raw meat equal in volume to a small creature. (Such as a gnome, which we hear are delicious with a little hot sauce.)

Champion Feat: You can take a recovery when your *lethal bite* attack staggers another creature or reduces it to 0 hit points.

Lethal bite: Your heavy jaw is powerful enough to crush bones to powder. When making an unarmed attack you deal 1d8 damage per level plus your Strength modifier. If you miss, you do 2 points of damage.

Adventurer Feat: On a natural 16+ hit with *lethal bite* your target is vulnerable to attacks by undead until the end of your next turn.

Champion Feat: On a natural even *lethal bite* attack roll against a vulnerable target, the target becomes stunned (save ends).

Epic Feat: Once per day as an immediate free action after making a *lethal bite* attack you gain a level-appropriate fear aura that lasts for the rest of the battle

GEARFORGED

Gain a +2 racial bonus to any one ability score

As you can see, the gearforged PC race is much more detailed than the optional Forgeborn/Dwarf-Forged PC race in 13th Age RPG, and anticipates at least a few of the questions about playing a living construct that could come up in play. ("Do I care that the ship's sinking? I can't drown, right?") You can find more ideas for playing a gearforged in **Advanced Races: Gearforged.**

Originally created as powerful soldiers, gearforged must now find their own paths with which to navigate the second life they have been given. Many devote themselves to civil service, others to their gods. Some dedicate their extraordinarily long lives to the pursuit of knowledge. Others, naturally, seek out lives of adventure.

METAL YET MORTAL (RACIAL POWER)

You are a living construct that houses a mortal soul. You don't need to eat, sleep or breathe, and you're immune to many conditions that affect those who continue to live in meat-bodies. But you do have other needs that they don't.

Brass and magic, not tissue and blood: Gearforged are immune to disease, ongoing damage from negative energy, ongoing damage from poison, and sleep effects.

Broken, not wounded: As machines, gearforged cannot heal on their own using recoveries, or take full heal-ups. But as living beings magically bound to machine bodies, they can heal using a recovery when they receive magical healing from spells, talents, potions or item powers—including *mending*, if the wizard casting it has taken the Cantrip Mastery talent. Gearforged can also heal using a recovery if another character with a background that includes building, maintaining and repairing gearforged makes a successful DC 20 check after spending an hour repairing the gearforged PC. The DC is reduced by 1 for every additional hour spent on repairs.

Champion Feat: You have a limited ability to repair yourself. You can heal using a recovery after an uninterrupted 4-hour maintenance period.

Epic Feat: You can now take advantage of full heal-ups, with no need for external magical aid to do so. The above rules for recoveries still apply.

Wrecked, not dead: You automatically stabilize when taken below 0 hit points or less. Your gearforged body is destroyed beyond repair if you die, and you cannot be raised or resurrected; but you can have your soul gem and memory tapes implanted in a newly constructed body as long as they are intact.

Amphibious: Gearforged do not need to breathe. A gearforged submerged in water can continue to function normally for a number of hours equal to their Strength score. After spending that much time in the water the gearforged will grind to a halt and requires a 4-hour repair period. Gearforged suffer a -4 penalty to swim checks.

Adventurer Feat: Design and training have made you far more effective in water than your gearforged fellows. Your lower body acts as a powerful and graceful propulsion system and your functioning is not impaired by long periods of submersion. You may operate underwater for as long as you like (though maintenance cannot be performed underwater and penalties from foregoing maintenance still apply) and you don't take a penalty to swim checks.

Champion Feat: You are fully equipped for aquatic combat and exploration. You can perform maintenance on yourself underwater, and you gain a +2 bonus to swim checks.

Tireless: Gearforged are immune to fatigue and exhaustion. Rather than sleep, gearforged must rewind their springs, repair gears, and oil and clean their parts each day for a 4-hour period to ensure normal functioning. They are fully aware during this period, but any interruption in their routine during these 4 hours requires them to start again from the beginning. Gearforged can function a number of days equal to their character level without performing this maintenance, but each day without such a repair period applies a cumulative −2 penalty on all attack and damage rolls and skill checks. If a gearforged neglects its maintenance period a number of days equal to his character level, it becomes immobile and helpless until maintained by another gearforged or an individual with an appropriate background. One 4-hour maintenance period eliminates all accumulated penalties.

Champion Feat: You only take a -1 cumulative penalty on skill checks, attack and damage rolls for each day without a 4-hour maintenance period.

Epic Feat: You have a state-of-the-art body that automatically maintains itself. You no longer take penalties when you go without daily maintenance, but the gear priests recommend maintenance every few months just to make sure everything's working properly.

GNOLLS

+2 Strength OR +2 Constitution

Desert raiders from the south, some gnolls become mercenaries or adventurers.

PACK ATTACK (RACIAL POWER)

If you are engaged with a target that an ally is also engaged with, add one extra damage die to a successful hit.

Champion Feat: Add the extra damage die to a miss as well.

Epic Feat: An ally who is engaged with an enemy that you are also engaged with can add one extra damage die to a hit or miss attack against that enemy.

GOBLINS OF THE WASTES

+2 Constitution OR +2 Intelligence OR +2 Wisdom

The goblin tribes will never be conquered, will never bend the knee. "Diplomat" and "treaty" are dirty words among goblinkind. Goblins choose to live free and on their own terms, even if that means living in the haunted and mage-blasted Wasted West. Never surrender! Freedom forever!

Or maybe they're just weird little creeps.

RACIAL POWERS

Your racial power comes from your tribe.

SPIRIT GUARDIAN (BONEWRAITH TRIBAL POWER)

When you become staggered you gain +2 to all its defenses until you are next hit.

Champion Feat: Bonus increases to +4 and you can make an immediate basic attack as a free action against the enemy who staggered you.

Epic Feat: When you become staggered you immediately deal 10 points damage to all nearby enemies.

SPEAKS WITH MACHINES (DUST DIGGER TRIBAL POWER)

Gain a +2 bonus to checks for understanding how a mechanical device works, and for sabotaging, disabling or repairing a mechanism. (Does not apply to living constructs.)

Champion Feat: Bonus increases to +4 and you gain a daily *cure wounds* spell (as a cleric of the same level) usable only on constructs.

Epic Feat: You realize that organic bodies are just another kind of machine! Your daily *cure wounds* spell is now usable on any living creature.

GHOST LIFE (GHOST GOBLIN TRIBAL POWER)

The first time you would be reduced to 0 hit points during a battle you are instead reduced to 5 hit points. If you are currently at 5 or fewer hit points, you take no damage.

Champion Feat: You also regenerate 5 hit points at the beginning of each turn until the end of the battle, or when you are next reduced to 0 hit points.

Epic Feat: If you are reduced to 0 hit points or less, have failed at least one death save, and you have at least one recovery left, you may use that recovery on your next turn to rise again as an undead ghost goblin. Start from 0 hit points and add the hit points you regained from using the recovery.

The following conditions will apply to you as an undead: You do not breathe, eat, or sleep or get tired. You are immune to ongoing poison damage, and to the confused, dazed, fear, stunned, and weakened effects. Negative energy damage heals you instead. Healing spells and potions do not affect you. You are vulnerable to holy attacks, and are affected by spells, attacks, abilities, talents and powers that target undead. If you are reduced to 0 hit points or less you are immediately destroyed (no death saves). You cannot be returned to life/undeath by anything that raises or reincarnates the dead. *Resurrection* returns you to life as a living goblin, not an undead one.

Kobolds

+2 Dexterity OR +2 Intelligence

Ever curious and quick to adapt to changing circumstances, kobolds have risen in this new world of cogs and gears. The brave little dragon-folk are miners, scouts, tinkerers, inventors, gearsmiths, alchemists... and some are also rogues and thieves. Above all, kobolds are survivors.

NIFTY FOOTWORK (RACIAL POWER)

When you miss with a melee attack you can pop free from the target as a free action. If you choose not to pop free you may add your Intelligence or Dexterity modifier to the damage of your next attack against this target.

Champion Feat: You can now also pop free from an enemy you're engaged with as a free action when that enemy's attack misses you. If you choose not to do so you may add 2x your Intelligence or Dexterity modifier to the next miss damage that you do this battle.

Epic Feat: You can now also pop free from an enemy you're engaged with as a free action when an ally engages that enemy. If you choose not to do so you may add 2x your Intelligence or Dexterity modifier to the next miss damage that you do this battle.

Kobold Adventurer Feat (Set Trap): Your missed attack was actually a clever ruse to maneuver your target into a hazard— you do 2x miss damage. If your attack normally has no miss damage, it does 2 miss damage.

Champion Tier Feat: Your target is also dazed until the end of their next turn.

Epic Tier Feat: Your target is also vulnerable until the end of their next turn.

KOBOLD SOBRIQUETS

You must spend at least one background point on your kobold sobriquet: the surname given to you by the kobold community because of a character trait, physical feature, occupation, great deed or shameful event. These canny survivors know the value of misdirection, so some sobriquets hide a kobold's true nature — a kobold named Takto Damnfool might leave you holding an empty coin purse in one hand and a worthless deed to the Puffing Bridge in the other.

Mechanically, a kobold sobriquet is simply a character background expressed as a name. But it's also public knowledge, so "Smaruk Backstabber" should expect to be treated with suspicion...

Minotaurs

+2 Strength OR +2 Wisdom

Many minotaurs carve their horns to show the deeds they have accomplished, such as solving mazes or killing a worthy foe. Minotaur mages are experts with labyrinthine magic - spells that trap others or confuse and misdirect enemies. Warrior minotaur often prefer a more direct head-on approach.

GORE (RACIAL POWER)

Your horns aren't just for decoration. Once per day you can add 1d6/level damage to a successful melee attack.

Champion Feat: *Gore* damage increases to 1d8/level.

Epic Feat: A *gored* target is also dazed.

RAVENFOLK (AKA HUGINN OR HERU)

+2 Dexterity OR +2 Wisdom

The ravenfolk are known as scoundrels and plotters; they are not entirely trusted, but have a reputation for never breaking an oath. Their homeland is Beldestan to the East, but they can be found on Wotan's tree and the high cliffs of the hidden temple of Horus in the South. They are known as heru or heriuti in the south, and huginn everywhere else.

WOTAN'S WISDOM (RACIAL POWER)
Once per battle you can reroll a natural even attack roll, or natural even skill check.
   Champion Feat: You can use *Wotan's wisdom* twice per battle.
   Epic Feat: You can now use *Wotan's wisdom* to grant an ally a reroll.

Ravenfolk Adventurer Feat (Carrion Crow): At one time you embraced the aspect of ravens as heralds of death and went to dwell among Midgard's undead. You returned with terrible knowledge. You gain a +2 bonus to knowledge skill checks related to undead, the Principality of Morgau and Doresh, and the Ghoul Imperium. You also gain a +2 bonus to AC against negative energy attacks.
   Champion Feat: The AC bonus increases to +4.
   Epic Feat: The AC bonus increases to +6 and you gain *turn undead* as the 1st level cleric spell. If you're already a cleric, gain an additional use of the spell per day.

Ravenfolk Champion Feat (Glide): You can fly at the rate you normally move until the end of your turn.
   Epic Feat: You can now fly until the end of your next turn.

Ravenfolk Adventurer Feat (Astounding Blade): Once per battle if you are using a sword in combat, you can deal 8 points damage to 1d3 nearby enemies as a quick action. If you're fighting mooks, add together any excess damage and apply it to any mooks left standing until you run out of damage, or run out of mooks.
   Champion Feat: You can deal 10 points damage to all nearby enemies as a quick action.
   Epic Feat: You can deal 15 points damage to all nearby enemies as a quick action.

Ravenfolk Adventurer Feat (Scion of Horus): You claim kinship with the hawk-headed god Horus, princely foe of ancient demons and their cults. Your crit range against demons and creatures in their service expands by 2 (normally 18+), and every attack you make deals holy damage instead of other types of damage unless you choose otherwise for a specific attack.
   Champion Feat: Your expanded crit range against demons and creatures in their service is now 4 (normally 16+).
   Epic Feat: Your expanded crit range against demons and creatures in their service is now 6 (normally 14+).

ROACHLINGS

+2 Dexterity OR +2 Constitution

The roachlings are a cursed people, found everywhere and always overlooked.

FOUR ARMED WARRIOR (RACIAL POWER)
If you roll a 2, 3, or 4 when making a melee weapon attack, you may reroll and take the second roll.
   Champion Feat: Your crit range on the reroll expands by 2.
   Epic Feat: Your crit range on the reroll expands by 4.

Roachling Champion Feat (Innate Survivor): Once per battle if you are dazed, you may immediately heal as though you spent a recovery.
   Epic Feat: This ability expands so you can use it when you are confused, dazed, hampered, stunned or weakened.

Roachling Champion Feat (Flexible Carapace): Whenever you are confused, dazed, hampered, stunned or weakened, you may immediately roll a hard save to end the condition.
   Epic Feat: You may now immediately roll a normal save against those conditions.

MIDGARD ICONS *by Wade Rockett*

INTRODUCTION

The Midgard Campaign Setting is a place of war and intrigue, where powerful figures pursue agendas that have roots in the distant past—in some cases, in the beginning of history. And as adventurers, you're right in the middle of their intrigues! Here are thirteen icons of Midgard and their suggested places on the Heroic, Ambiguous and Villainous scale.

Unlike the icons presented in the *13th Age* RPG, the Midgard icons vary wildly in power and scope of influence. The Queen of Night and Magic is a goddess. The Dragon Sultana rules a mighty empire. The King of Bears leads a remote kingdom, and the Free City Council governs a city-state. But Midgard's long history, vibrant trade and deep magic connects them all and extends their reach. The Beloved Imperatrix cares about the price of grain in Zobeck, and a prisoner on Demon Mountain might find unexpected help from a hero on an errand for Baba Yaga.

BABA YAGA

A hunched crone with iron teeth and a ferocious gaze, Baba Yaga has existed for as long as anyone remembers; she may be as old as the world. "Grandmother" is a hoarder of secrets and a powerful fey who makes it her business to know everything. She flies through the air in a mortar, wielding a pestle, and has aided or destroyed some of history's greatest heroes and villains.

BELOVED IMPERATRIX

Regia Moonthorn Kalthania-Reln van Dornig is an ancient elven woman who speaks in a whisper that can carry the length of a ballroom, and she moves with a quiet grace.

DRAGON SULTANA

The Dragon Sultana's rule is new and fragile, but she has the confidence and the ruthlessness needed to command the mighty draconic Mharoti Empire.

EMPEROR OF THE GHOULS

Nicoforus the Pale is the undisputed ruler of the Dread and Endless Imperium of the Darakhul, a civilization of ghouls deep within the realms subterranean. Through cunning and relentless cruelty he's led his legions to repeated victories over the other races in the underworld. Drow, dwarves, kobolds, gnomes – all are slaves or food for the darakhul. Only the ghouls' aversion to the sun keeps the Imperium from invading the surface world.

EXARCH VERMES II

Exarch Vermes II is one of the most influential and mysterious figures in Bemmea, a city riddled with mysteries. The inhuman wizard who leads its Ninemage Council has molded his city for centuries into the place it is today.

FIRST DUKE-ADMIRAL CADUA

The first minotaur to serve as First Duke-Admiral of Triolo, Cadua is a polarizing figure. Some consider the "Golden Horn" a promising sign of Kyprion's and Triolo's joint destiny. Others feel sure that he steers the Maritime Republic to ruin.

FREE CITY COUNCIL

Drawn from all walks of life, the 12 members of the Free City Council ensure the welfare of Zobeck and its citizens, protect it from all threats to its freedom, and maintain the flow of commerce.

GLITTERING KING

The Glittering King is steeped in luxury and wine: a paranoid drunkard with a great temper and tremendous power over his terrified nobles. His mastery of dark magic and fleet of demon ships makes his slave kingdom into a force that few dare challenge.

ILLUMINATED BROTHERHOOD

This esoteric society is open to all dwarves who qualify and seek perfection in their chosen craft. Many high-ranking members of dwarven society, including some kings, count themselves among the ranks of the Illuminated Brotherhood.

KING OF BEARS

The King of Bears rules the bears and lycanthropes of the North, served by a cadre of witches and oracles. His royal court spends most of its time hunting, feasting, brawling, and drinking the finest honey mead from immense stone bowls.

MASTER OF DEMON MOUNTAIN

The Master of Demon Mountain's spells and incantations carry great potency. The demons praise him, and his many children are tiefling ambassadors to the world, heralds of his power. But his real goal is to reach immortality—although first he must break the pacts binding him to Demon Mountain.

ORACLE OF KAMMAE

The blind daughter of the moon is blessed — or cursed — with divine insight, and gifts of healing and prophecy. With the voices of spirits, angels, and canny counselors around her, the Oracle of Kammae Straboli rarely errs in matters of fact or faith.

QUEEN OF NIGHT AND MAGIC

The Queen of Night and Magic rules the Shadow Realm, where she dreams of conquest, blood, and loss. She remembers too many worlds that once were hers.

HEROIC, AMBIGUOUS OR VILLAINOUS?

Here's how the icons are presented in in the Midgard Campaign Setting. Feel free to decide that in your own campaign Baba Yaga is a friend to heroes, or that the Dragon Sultana is a good and just monarch presiding over (or fighting to bring about) a golden age.

Heroic Icons: Usually First Duke-Admiral Cadua, the King of Bears, the Beloved Imperatrix, the Illuminated Brotherhood, the Free City Council; possibly Exarch Vermes II.

Ambiguous Icons: Usually Baba Yaga, the Oracle of Kammae, Exarch Vermes II, the Dragon Sultana; possibly the Queen of Night and Magic and the Illuminated Brotherhood.

Villainous Icons: Usually the Ghoul Emperor, the Queen of Night and Magic, the Glittering King, the Master of Demon Mountain; possibly Baba Yaga and the Oracle of Kammae.

BABA YAGA

A hunched crone with iron teeth and a ferocious gaze, Baba Yaga has existed for as long as anyone remembers; she may be as old as the world. "Grandmother" is a hoarder of secrets and a powerful fey who makes it her business to know everything. She flies through the air in a mortar, wielding a pestle, and has aided or destroyed some of history's greatest heroes and villains.

QUOTE

"Very well: if you take good care of my mares, I'll give you a heroic steed. But if you don't, then you mustn't be annoyed at finding your head stuck on top of that pole there."

USUAL LOCATION

Baba Yaga lives in a hut that wanders throughout Midgard on enormous chicken legs, though it most often frequents the Central Heart of the Old Margreve forest and the wide reaches of the Rothenian Plain. It permits entry only to those who address it politely.

COMMON KNOWLEDGE

There are many tales of Baba Yaga; most contradict each other. It's hard to get a sense of Old Boney Legs, and one suspects that's exactly what she wants.

All the mortal lands, the lords of heaven and hell, and the very gods themselves leave the Fell Crone to herself out of fear. The knowledge she possesses could easily destroy the most powerful of entities. She is content with simply knowing, but she will gladly demolish those foolish enough to test her: Many have been erased from history for their wasted efforts to best her.

Baba Yaga is the consummate schemer, always a hundred steps ahead of the opposition with contingencies in place for even the most outlandish of possibilities. The wise let her be.

ADVENTURERS AND THE ICON

Baba Yaga is a trader of secrets. The brave, the desperate, and the stupid often make pilgrimages to seek her wisdom, though she inevitably tries to force them into her service—often transformed into a beast of burden or common tool—or simply eats them.

She parts with her knowledge only for a price: perhaps a first kiss, a final breath, or a forgotten artifact. For those capable of tricking her, anything in the multiverse is within reach.

Those very few who possess knowledge that she wants have a rare sway over her, for she will offer much to own it—though it's still best not to push her too far. She never forgets a slight, as the gnomes of Midgard learned to their dismay.

ALLIES

The Glittering King owes his success to Baba Yaga, and her veela daughter Eldara is one of his favorites. The Feywitch is always welcome in the Queen of Night's court, and the Oracle of Kammae has a mystical connection to Baba Yaga through the mysteries of Hecate.

ENEMIES

Baba Yaga's dealings with the deposed Stross family of Zobeck make her a foe of the Free City Consul, and the Bear King of the North holds a long-standing grudge against her that he angrily refuses to discuss.

HISTORY

No one knows where Baba Yaga came from or how old she is, but her name appears throughout the annals of Midgard, in every corner of the world:

- Baba Yaga gave the Black Sorceress the incantations and True Names used in the Great Revolt to shatter and corrupt Midgard's fey roads.
- She warned the vampire prince Lucan about the good cleric Kjord, prompting him to crush his foe and cement his dark rule over Morgau.
- Midgard's gnomes became slaves of the arch-devils of the Eleven Hells to escape Baba Yaga's wrath.
- Ancient tales say the Kalder, the Black Gypsies who serve Chernovog, were born from Baba Yaga's cauldron.
- She taught Veltrin the Glittering King the art of commanding demons, making his demon ship *Golden Bird* the flagship of a mighty slaver fleet.
- The grand duchess of Illyria used brass shackles enchanted by Baba Yaga to bind the captured dragon Zrandres.

Grandmother appears in many places at once, as if there were more than one crone of the same name. She often mentions her sisters; perhaps they are identical twins who respond to the same name. It might also be that her "sisters" are echoes of Baba Yaga in time.

Baba Yaga is sometimes found with her daughters, the beautiful fey known as veela. They do her bidding, but they sometimes take pity on her victims and help them.

Other servants include Koschei the Deathless, a gaunt, pallid sorcerer who rides a black mare and is the incarnation of death itself; and her three horsemen, Bright Day, Red Sun, and Black Night, who act as her emissaries, scouts, and warriors. Her hut is filled with former petitioners she's transformed into talking animals and household tools. They serve her, but might betray her if a guest treats them kindly.

THE TRUE DANGER

Everything will be all right provided that nobody provokes Baba Yaga to a revenge so terrible that it unravels reality itself.

BELOVED IMPERATRIX

Regia Moonthorn Kalthania-Reln van Dornig is an ancient elven woman who speaks in a whisper that can carry the length of a ballroom, and she moves with a quiet grace.

QUOTE

"Come closer, child. Why, I can see your great-great-great-great-grandfather in your eyes, and in the set of your jaw. How is he?"

USUAL LOCATION

The Court of the Beloved Imperatrix has no set place. Instead, it moves between the three largest cities of the Grand Duchy. This Great Procession is a mammoth undertaking, moving the Imperatrix, her personal retinue, a court of some 400 courtiers, their personal entourage, and a variety of support personnel. The Great Procession takes place every three years, after the harvest and before the start of the Court Season.

COMMON KNOWLEDGE

The southern kingdoms squabble over who is the true heir of the ancient elven empires, but in the north there is no doubt. The Grand Duchy of Dornig, also known as the Domains of the Princes, is the one truly successor state to the power that once was Arbonesse and Thorn. This is most evident in their ruler. Upon the Copper Sphinx Throne of Dornig sits one of the few elves who remembers the Age of Glory, before the Great Retreat, and before the despoliations of the Great Mage Wars. She is the Beloved Imperatrix Regia Moonthorn Kalthania-Reln vann Dornig, and all of this land's lesser rulers, by blood and by marriage, are her children.

Gifted with the presence of a singular respected ruler, her realm should be a land of peace and prosperity. But it is a land of continual political intrigue, as the three most powerful branches of Kalthania's descendants—and a host of minor cadet branches—plot and conspire against each other. When the Imperatrix is awake and aware, she rules fairly and justly. However, she is now in her fifth century, venerable even by elven standards, and she often nods and leaves the duties to her descendants.

ADVENTURERS AND THE ICON

The Imperatrix rarely turns to non-elf adventurers for aid—at least publicly. In reality, she secretly employs many agents from other races. Some of them long for a mythical "golden age" in which wise and noble elves protected Midgard, and the nations were at peace. Others are just happy to accept the elves' gold. The Imperatrix might send adventurers to retrieve a magic item or imperial heirloom, rescue a spy from danger, or tip the balance of power toward the elves in ways that can't easily be traced back to them.

ALLIES

The Imperatrix and the Queen of Night and Magic are all that remain of the elves' ancient glory in Midgard; and, well, family is family.

ENEMIES

The Imperatrix and the Illuminated Brotherhood reject each other's claim to Grisal, which was ruled as part of the Grand Duchy of Dornig by elfmarked members of House Hirsch-Dammung until the dwarves took the territory to prevent it from falling into the hands of Prince Lucan of Morgau and Doresh. Although Exarch Vermes II visits the Imperatrix each year to pay his respects on her birthday, relations between the two are strained at best.

HISTORY

Some say that it was the rising power of the humans that caused the Archons of the Elves to abandon these lands. Other sources say the humans found something that caused the elves to flee. Still others speak of betrayal by the shadow elves that caused the Last Horn to be sounded. Even the elves and elfmarked of the current age know only whispers of the past, rumors changed and altered with time. Only one surviving elf knows the truth of the matter.

She is the elf who stayed behind when the rest of Archon's Court chose to pilgrimage back to Elfheim: Regia Kalthania, called Moonthorn by the Company of the Blessed, with whom she traveled. When her human companion Reln vann Dornig's family was slain by a group of diabolists seeking to use Dornig as a base, Reln, Moonthorn, and their allies defeated the diabolists, and Reln took both the crown of Dornig and Moonthorn as his consort. She in turn took the name of Regia Moonthorn Kalthania-Reln, Baroness of Dornig. Over time the Baroness became a Duchess and then a Grand Duchess, and at last became the Imperatrix of the Grand Duchy.

Her rule has been peaceful, for the most part. Yet as the Imperatrix continues her long reign and is now within sight of her Fifth Jubilee, the houses great and small wonder what will happen after she does pass. And many are preparing for that eventuality.

THE TRUE DANGER

Everything will be all right as long as the Beloved Imperatrix's descendants don't tire of waiting for her to name an heir to the throne, and decide to determine the matter themselves.

DRAGON SULTANA

The Dragon Sultana's rule is new and fragile, but she has the confidence and the ruthlessness needed to command the mighty draconic Mharoti Empire.

QUOTE

"I rule in the name of the Scaled Lords, in the name of Mharot and Veles. To stand in my presence is to stand with the coils of the World Serpent about you."

USUAL LOCATION

In the Golden City of Harkesh, at the Imperial Palace of the Eight Elements.

COMMON KNOWLEDGE

The vastly powerful Mharoti Empire was founded by dragons and is run by dragons for their enrichment. It is one of the few places where humans and their kin are distinctly second-class citizens, though there is one notable exception: The dragons choose not to appoint one of their own to rule the empire. Their vanity was such that they could never agree on a dragon ruler, so they gave the job to a clearly inferior species instead. The Empire is ruled by a human sultan or sultana, who loosely holds the reins of power.

The charismatic, 26-year-old Dragon Sultana Casmara Azrabahir stands a mere 5 feet tall but radiates the aura of command that one would expect from the ruler of the world's mightiest empire, whose position is backed by dragons. She is a skilled sorcerer whose color-streaked black hair confirms her Chromatic Destroyer Heritage — and she has been known to exhibit the creature's foul temperament, as well. The Dragon Sultana can also fascinate dragons and dragon-kin with her voice.

ADVENTURERS AND THE ICON

Most adventures that involve the Dragon Sultana also involve the affairs of dragonkind, from kobolds to dragonkin to drakes. Those that involve the Great Dragon Lords themselves are the most dangerous and most lucrative. Adventurers may be recruited by the Dragon Sultana or her organization to help resolve issues of nesting rituals, peculiar forms of status or insult, or assassination of seemingly inconsequential personages — or they may become embroiled at the highest levels in court intrigue or even a naked power grab.

ALLIES

The Glittering King pays tribute to the Dragon Sultana, and she has given private audiences to Baba Yaga of late — though none know what they might be planning.

ENEMIES

The Dragon Sultana's plans for imperial expansion include control of the seas, and First Duke-Admiral Cadua of Triolo is determined to see that she doesn't get it.

HISTORY

Two years ago the young Sultana Casmara Azrabahir murdered her weak, dragon-bloodless uncle Sultan Abdrazin Azrabahir and assumed control of the Empire. The sultan's elite palace guards—the Order of the Wyvern—fell quickly in line, not questioning her usurpation, but some dragons, drakes, and emirs are still squabbling about whether to stand for or against the new order. The sultana has powerful allies within their ranks, and so has turned her attention away from possible coups and toward expansion.

If the Dragon Sultana didn't exist, the Mharoti Empire would not be an empire—it would more closely resemble eight draconic kingdoms at war. The young Sultana Casmara has a great deal of power, but only because the governors don't trust any of their own number with that much authority. And yet, she plans effectively and commands the imperial legions and the morza (a draconic term that translates roughly as "prince" or "dragon governor" or "great lord"). The threat of swift, silent death at the hands of the Dragon Sultana's harem assassins is usually enough to keep dragonkin and human satraps in line.

The Dragon Sultana has had little time to enjoy the privileges that come with her role, but rumors swirl that the Royal Harem might soon see a swath of handsome male consorts.

THE TRUE DANGER

Everything will be all right as long as the Dragon Sultana cannot achieve her goal of conquering Nuria Natal and plundering its ancient secrets.

EMPEROR OF THE GHOULS

Nicoforus the Pale is the undisputed ruler of the Dread and Endless Imperium of the Darakhul, a civilization of ghouls deep within the realms subterranean. Through cunning and relentless cruelty he's led his legions to repeated victories over the other races in the underworld. Drow, dwarves, kobolds, gnomes – all are slaves or food for the darakhul. Only the ghouls' aversion to the sun keeps the Imperium from invading the surface world.

QUOTE
"Rejoice, meat: you will have the honor of feeding our royal person."

USUAL LOCATION
In the White City of Darakhan, or in his pleasure palace at Vandekhul on the shore of the Sulphur Sea.

COMMON KNOWLEDGE
The Imperium is an undead civilization fueled by inhuman hunger and animal fury. It works tirelessly to extend its power, fighting an eternal war against all that lives and breathes. Well-hidden, it has bided its time for a century, growing in strength, in knowledge, and in numbers.

Nicoforus the Pale is the emperor of this grim, charnel realm.

The few living creatures who have seen him and survived report that he appears as a man of middle years, his hair black and his flesh as white as ivory, wearing purple and black clothes and a silvery crown set with emeralds. He never goes anywhere without his two bodyguards and four personal servants, and is usually accompanied by a retinue of scribes, priests, powerful merchants, council members, and an honor guard of 20 Iron Ghouls. All ghouls revere their emperor as almost godlike, and they will protect him fanatically.

ADVENTURERS AND THE ICON
Nicoforus trusts the arcane powers more than the divine ones of the various high priests, and under his rule the masters of necromancy known as the necrophagi prosper. Despite a constant risk that their hosts may forget their manners and eat them, necromancers leap at any opportunity to study death magic at the fane of the necrophagi in Darakhan.

Evil clerics of the death god Anu-Akma, the hunger god Vardesain (known to humans as Mordiggian), the war god Mavros, and the Goddess of Night and Magic may seek out the Ghoul Emperor, as do those diabolists whose rites include carrion and cannibalism.

ALLIES
The Queen of the Shadow Fey would receive Nicoforus as a guest if he cared to call, and she maintains an embassy in Darakhan. His slaughter of the drow marks him as her enemy, but the pragmatic queen prefers to manipulate the Ghoul Emperor rather than attempt to destroy him.

The Archwizard of Bemmea understands the Ghoul Emperor well, having magic and long life in common. The Glittering King of the Slavers of Reth-Saal does not much care where his wares end up and the Imperium's need for slaves is never-ending.

ENEMIES
Ultimately all living, sane beings oppose the plans of the Ghoul Emperor.

HISTORY
Four great emperors have ruled the ghouls, giving homage to the Death God Anu-Akma and to Mordiggian, the Demon Lord of Ghouls, also called Vardesain.

For the past twenty years, Nicoforus the Pale has held the empire together through cunning and relentless cruelty. He took revenge on the drow for his predecessor's death by assassinating the high priestess of their largest city and then destroying it utterly. His legions took all dark elves in the city prisoner, eating the weak and transforming the strongest into ghouls.

THE TRUE DANGER
Everything will be all right provided that the Ghoul Emperor never finds a way to overcome his legions' vulnerability to sunlight.

EXARCH VERMES II

Exarch Vermes II is one of the most influential and mysterious figures in Bemmea, a city riddled with mysteries. The inhuman wizard who leads its Ninemage Council has molded his city for centuries into the place it is today.

QUOTE

"Mastery of magic is mastery of the world."

USUAL LOCATION

In Bemmea's Spire Perilous, presiding over the Council that rules the Magocracy of Allain in the Wasted West.

COMMON KNOWLEDGE

The spire that houses the Council of Caelmarath rises from atop the highlands of the Bemmean peninsula, at the terminus of the long Mage Road. From here, nine archmages of unfathomable power rule the magocracy of Allain.

Over them all looms Vermes II, the Exarch of Bemmea. Rumors swirl around this ancient wizard. Some claim he is the last pureblooded Ankeshelian. Others call him a half-demon bred from Caelmarath royalty. Old stories hold that beneath his face-shrouding robes is a writhing inhuman form.

Within the Spire Perilous the members of the Ninemage Council scheme and plot in an ancient dance of unusual rules, obscure transgressions, and bizarre rituals. The Exarch subtly manipulates this collection of egos and eccentricities to ensure that things don't get out of hand. His influence keeps simmering rivalries from boiling over into all-out magical war—though he turns a blind eye to the occasional duel that occurs as a way of relieving pressure.

ADVENTURERS AND THE ICON

The Exarch's missions often involve the weird and horrific, pitting adventurers against forgotten cults and mind-shattering alien horrors. But the Exarch plays a deep and complicated game. Adventurers working for him rarely discover the true effect their quests have on the world until years later, if at all. If they're lucky, the Exarch's true opponents never learn their names.

The Gathering of Thoth-Hermes, a midwinter fair of arcanists and bookbinders, draws Midgard's sorcerers, wizards, and occultists (with a smattering of clerics) to Bemmea each year. The Exarch will sometimes take advantage of this gathering to hire adventurers for tasks he cannot entrust to local mages.

ALLIES

The Exarch sometimes visits the Master of Demon Mountain and the Courts of the Shadow Fey on matters magical and political, and calls upon Baba Yaga at her hut every New Year's Dawn. (A bawdy Bemmean tavern song speculates at length on the nature of this annual meeting, though we will not offend our readership's refined sensibilities by reproducing it here.)

The Exarch and the Ghoul Emperor have come to a mutual understanding, and their official representatives are granted safe passage through their respective realms.

ENEMIES

Although the Exarch visits the Imperatrix of Dornig each year to pay his respects on her birthday, relations between the two are strained at best. The Exarch and Bloodmother Margase have a well-practiced loathing of one another; and the Mharoti Dragons and the Sultana have their own designs, often at odds with the Exarch, and rarely appreciate his meddling in their affairs.

HISTORY

The Exarch has ruled Bemmea since the days of the Mage War, and was vital in preserving and rebuilding the Magocracy. Indeed, the Wasted West would be even more horrific were it not for the Exarch's efforts. He is no stranger to the dark paths of magic—but there are much worse out there, and the Exarch's magic keeps them (mostly) in check.

Eighty years ago, the Exarch destroyed the conspiracy responsible for the Hakren Affair, in which a cabal of demon-influenced scribes assassinated their master by creating enchanted ink and words that turned against the mage and strangled him. More than half of the Council was killed by glyph magic before the Exarch's divinations exposed the perpetrators. They burned in arcane fire.

THE TRUE DANGER

Everything will be all right as long as the Exarch is able to prevent ambitious wizards from reawakening the Great Old Ones.

FIRST DUKE-ADMIRAL CADUA

The first minotaur to serve as First Duke-Admiral of Triolo, Cadua is a polarizing figure. Some consider the "Golden Horn" a promising sign of Kyprion's and Triolo's joint destiny. Others feel sure that he steers the Maritime Republic to ruin.

QUOTE

"My lord, I will accept your surrender or send you and your fleet to the hell of your choosing. I suggest you decide quickly."

USUAL LOCATION

In Triolo, at the Ducal Manor or in the Forum of the Golden Council.

COMMON KNOWLEDGE

The Golden Council of merchant families governs Triolo, but much of its policy is in the hands of the commanders of its fleet. They are led by the First Duke-Admiral, whom the Council elects to serve for life or until he or she abdicates the position.

First Duke-Admiral Cadua inspires loyalty in his followers, fear in his foes, and respect in all. His appearance alone astonishes those who are not prepared for it: a minotaur dressed in an admiral's finery, with one horn replaced by a horn of gold, one hand replaced by a seaman's hook, and one eye covered by an embroidered patch.

Failure, injury and even death hold no terror for the First Duke-Admiral: he has been through the fire and emerged victorious. Now he leads his people and his fleet with sharp intelligence, courage and hard-won wisdom. Cadua faces adversity in all its forms with a wry humor and fierce determination.

ADVENTURERS AND THE ICON

There are plenty of opportunities for adventure, fortune and glory with Triolo's legendary corsairs. The First Duke-Admiral doesn't shy away from piracy, but he will not tolerate cowardice, treachery or needless cruelty in those who serve with him. Success in a mission sponsored by the First Duke-Admiral will earn you a free drink in many a seaside tavern. It will also make you extremely unpopular with those who've lost ships to the corsairs.

ALLIES

The "Golden Horn" and the Bear King share a great mutual respect and affection. The First Duke-Admiral and Zobeck's Free City Council are sometimes rivals in trade, and sometimes allies against those who would halt or oppress the hard-working merchant-pirate classes.

ENEMIES

The Sultana's Mharoti Empire is the only sea power formidable enough to contest Triolo's dominance of the waves; and the Oracle of Kammae and the First Duke-Admiral maintain a long-standing feud over the enslavement of the sea god Nethus. The hatred between the First Duke-Admiral and the Glittering King goes well beyond the rivalry between their nations: their final duel, whether it's ship to ship or blade versus blade, will be legendary.

HISTORY

As an impetuous youth, Captain Cadua led several Triolan ships into a Mharoti trap and barely escaped with his scars. Shamed, he was told he would never command a ship again, since he lacked the wisdom to lead.

Cadua left Triolo to find that wisdom, and he did, for a terrible price. He visited each oracle across the length and breadth of the land. To the Clockwork Oracle, he lost a horn; to the God-Slavers of Kammae, he gave an eye; and to the Spider Oracle of the Southlands, he sacrificed a hand in exchange for insight.

A scant five years later, Cadua returned to Triolo, burning with the faith of Mavros and leading a score of ships. The people of Triolo, even his detractors, acclaim him as the first and greatest of the minotaurs, and they acknowledge his potential to lead his people into the highest ranks of Triolo's navy and society.

THE TRUE DANGER

Everything will be all right as long as the First Duke-Admiral's wisdom does not desert him, leading the Maritime Republic to disaster and giving the Mharoti Empire command of the seas.

FREE CITY COUNCIL

Drawn from all walks of life, the 12 members of the Free City Council ensure the welfare of Zobeck and its citizens, protect it from all threats to its freedom, and maintain the flow of commerce.

QUOTE

"When you leave the building, turn left and continue until you find the headquarters of the sub-sub-subcommittee in charge of Grievances Involving Medium-Sized Pack Animals. I assure you, Baron, that they will pursue your case with the zeal and diligence that it deserves."

USUAL LOCATION

In the Council Hall in Upper Zobeck.

COMMON KNOWLEDGE

To visitors and newcomers, Zobeck's government is a many-layered nightmare of bureaucracy, hidden connections and unspoken rules for getting things done. However, it provides the city with security and safety for trade; justice and fair dealings in the markets; and to the poor, work as conscripts or ditchdiggers. The Free City Council sits atop its hierarchy, where it has served Zobeck since the Great Revolt.

Generally descendants of the Great Revolt's leaders, the 12 members of the Free City Council serve for life or until they retire. Sitting Consuls fill any vacancies from among the city's most prominent civic leaders: typically guildmasters, merchants, or powerful members of the priesthood. Once in a while, the Consuls choose a prominent adventurer who seeks a quieter life.

The sitting Consuls select the Lord Mayor from among their peers to serve a 10-year term, though most have held the position for life. The Lord Mayor appoints Zobeck's judges and knight-commanders of the Citadel, establishes and provisions the army, and commands the Free City's militant orders—except the paladins of the Order of the Undying Sun, which predates the city's independence.

A secret council known as the Praetors serves as the Lord Mayor's eyes, ears, and hands throughout the city. The Praetors are the core of Zobeck's secret police network, indirectly controlling the city's internal and external spies, jailers, and tax collectors. The number of Praetors never exceeds five, and Consuls sometimes also serve as Praetors. The identity of the Praetorians typically remains secret.

Current Consuls

- Karillian Gluck, Lord Mayor
- Ondli Firedrake, First Consul and High Priest of Rava-Among-the-Dwarves and Volund
- Kuromak, Kobold King of Kings*
- Radovar Streck, City Consul
- Melancha Vendemic, City Consul
- Kekolina of the Derry Mine, City Consul
- Myzi I, Mouse King
- Orlando, Guildmaster of the Arcane Collegium
- Lord Volstaff Greymark, master merchant and Consul
- Lady Wintesla Marack, master merchant of House Marack and Consul
- Halsen Hrovitz IV, master merchant of House Hrovitz and Consul
- Azeleanara Perunisis, retired adventurer originally from the Duchy of Perun's Daughter

This seat's Consul fluctuates with the rise and fall of the Kobold King of Kings in the Kobold Ghetto; Kuromak is the seat's sixth holder in the last two years.

ADVENTURERS AND THE ICON

Zobeck's freedom comes with a price, and that price is trouble. Whether it's clockwork constructs running amok, an invasion by the Shadow Fey, wars between rival street gangs or riots in the Kobold Ghetto, the Free City Council often turns to outside help in dealing with the latest crisis. But Zobeck is also a city of secrets and shadows, and seemingly straightforward jobs can get complicated fast.

ALLIES

The Free City Council and First Duke-Admiral Cadua of Triolo are commercial rivals; but they are formidable military allies against any foe who threatens their mutual interests. As long as the Illuminated Brotherhood doesn't threaten the authority of the Free City Council, the two are united in preserving Zobeck against its foes.

ENEMIES

The Ghoul Emperor is a constant threat to the safety of Zobeck and its citizens. And however much the Free City Council enjoys the benefits of trade with the Winter Court, it doesn't change the fact that the Queen of Night and Magic was the power behind the nobility who ruled Zobeck in the old, bad days.

HISTORY

The Free City Council replaced the House Stross-era Praetorian Council after the Revolt. Once composed of hand picked noble allies of House Stross, the Praetorian Council spent most of their time scheming and plotting against one another. They pilfered money from the city to fund their own projects, ruinously taxed the city's bourgeoisie, restricted trade with tariffs and exit fees, and used the Watch as their personal enforcers. This flagrant corruption laid the groundwork for the violence that destroyed the old aristocracy.

After the Great Revolt, the rebels imprisoned or executed any Praetorian Council members they caught. The Revolt's leaders created the Free City Council to administer the city as the Praetorian Council should have done. Its standing Consul members were citizens who helped lead the Revolt and who held strong interests in the city–mostly guildmasters, priests, and even kobolds.

By tradition, the Free City Council always includes the Guildmaster of the Arcane Collegium and the Kobold King of Kings. During the Revolt, the leaders gave the city's Watch commander a lifetime council seat but secretly decided that, unlike the deal they struck with the kobolds and the Arcane Collegium, this "seat for life" would only extend to that individual. Upon his death, the Council did not give the position to his successor but added a second seat for a cleric of Rava. To this day, this "betrayal" remains a point of contention between the Council and the Watch.

THE TRUE DANGER

Everything will be all right as long as the Free City's volatile mix of political factions, humanoid races, cults, criminal gangs, merchant guilds and military orders continues to exist in (relative) peace.

GLITTERING KING

The Glittering King is steeped in luxury and wine: a paranoid drunkard with a great temper and tremendous power over his terrified nobles. His mastery of dark magic and fleet of demon ships makes his slave kingdom into a force that few dare challenge.

QUOTE

"Ahh. I see that you recognize the one who stands guard at my side. I would have him greet his old friends properly, but I'm afraid he is not much of a conversationalist these days."

USUAL LOCATION

Within his jeweled palace at Reth-Saal, or aboard his demon flagship the Golden Bird.

COMMON KNOWLEDGE

The name of Veltrin the Younger, Glittering King and Despot of the Ruby Sea, is lavished with fawning praise within his kingdom but is a curse among the free folk of the Rothenian Plains. His subjects are debauched and sadistic slavers who will sell to anyone: the gnomes, the tsar, the priests of Baal, and even to the Ghoul Emperor.

By offering blood sacrifices to the White Goddess, the Glittering King can create an army of fearsome proportions in a matter of days, magically turning his slaves into monstrous, bloodthirsty warriors. These warriors all die a short time later, but the King considers his own safety and well-being worth the cost.

In recent years, the Glittering King has taken to wearing a mithral mask studded with sapphires, rubies, and chalcedony. He raids his neighbors with increasing regularity, and his grip on the Despotate tightens even as its debauchery grows wilder.

ADVENTURERS AND THE ICON

The Glittering King and his wealthy, decadent nobles crave wealth and power. They often hire mercenaries to seek after hidden treasure, powerful items of black magic, or information that will ensure victory in an upcoming raid. Only the vilest creatures willingly serve such masters.

ALLIES

The Glittering King pays "loyal" tribute to the Dragon Sultana because hers is the only nation that could crush him. Baba Yaga's daughter Eldara is a favorite in his court, and he enjoys a highly profitable trade selling slaves to the Ghoul Emperor and the Gnome King.

ENEMIES

First Duke-Admiral Cadua of Triolo would happily end the Glittering King's life with a sweep of his axe, and sail back to Triolo with the Despot's head nailed to the prow.

HISTORY

The slaving fleet of the Rubeshi is widely feared, and the secret of its success is its flagship, the *Golden Bird*. The figurehead at its prow is a bound demon named Yarochort, a horrific figure draped in rusty chains.

Veltrin the Elder, the Glittering King's father, found the figurehead in a wreck washed ashore. He had no idea how to command it, so he learned the secrets of binding and controlling demons from Baba Yaga and the Master of Demon Mountain. Thus empowered, Veltrin and his single pirate ship took slaves by the score.

Hungry to become more than just another pirate captain, he began to assemble an entire fleet and put those slaves whom he did not sell to work laying the foundation stones of the city of Reth-Saal. Those who could not work were fed to demons. When Veltrin the Elder died, his son inherited all and became the Glittering King.

During the Boyar's Rebellion, a dozen of the Glittering King's ship captains and one of his generals plotted to murder him. The Glittering King executed the plotters, then stitched their bodies into the first of the Elect: 50 flesh golems who serve as his bodyguards. Creating them took years and a fortune, but seeing former generals and powerful galley commanders jump at his every word amuses the Glittering King still, and terrifies his enemies. No coup has been attempted since.

THE TRUE DANGER

Everything will be all right as long as the Dragon Sultana can keep the Glittering King's depredations in check.

ILLUMINATED BROTHERHOOD

This esoteric society is open to all dwarves who qualify and seek perfection in their chosen craft. Many high-ranking members of dwarven society, including some kings, count themselves among the ranks of the Illuminated Brotherhood.

QUOTE

"I repeat my question, friend—and I suggest you consider your answer carefully. Are you, then, a Craftsman?"

USUAL LOCATION

Members of the Illuminated Brotherhood congregate weekly in great meeting halls in any settlement with a significant population of dwarven craftsmen. The centerpiece of dwarven life in many communities, these great halls are extravagant and often gaudy displays of rich excess.

COMMON KNOWLEDGE

Originally formed to protect dwarven trading secrets and strengthen moral character among its members, the Illuminated Brotherhood has grown into a mysterious and powerful secret society. Outsiders often accuse the order of hiding terrible secrets and negotiating behind-the-scenes manipulations of craft guilds and government.

Outside their lodges, members of the order go to great lengths to conceal their membership in the brotherhood to outsiders, especially non-dwarves, and appear as ordinary members of their professions. Only the most subtle hints of their involvement might give away their membership to other brothers in the society. Often, a simple ring embossed with a runic "B," a belt of golden chain, or a spinning fob are the only indication of membership. In addition, members know certain markers, most predominantly secret handshakes and specific cadences tapped out by the hot hammers of the forge, that broadcast their membership to other initiates of the order.

ADVENTURERS AND THE ICON

Few non-dwarf adventurers outside the Brotherhood ever come in contact with it—in fact, few even know it exists unless they have a background in a craft guild. However, most dwarves have at least one relative in the society. There's always a chance that a dwarf adventurer will receive a mysterious late-night visitor who displays a sign of the order, and invokes the powerful bonds of kinship to ask a favor.

ALLIES

The Free City Council is on good terms with the Illuminated Brotherhood as long as it doesn't flex its muscles too much in city politics, or disrupt free trade.

ENEMIES

The Illuminated Brotherhood is committed to containing the threat of the Ghoul Emperor. The Beloved Imperatrix of Dornig rejects the claim of the dwarves to Grisal, the Black Canton; the Brotherhood is firmly on the side of those dwarves who insist that dwarven rule is necessary to keep the undead at bay.

HISTORY

Most groups of the Illuminated Brotherhood operate under the moral codes of the Great Founding Fathers, while operating with independent jurisdiction and welcoming members of other groups openly. Members congregate weekly in their halls to share knowledge and study their unique system of principles, veiled in lessons of morality taught through symbolism and allegory, which they call the Craft.

As members learn these lessons and apply them to their livelihoods, the brotherhood awards them progressions of accomplishment known as degrees, of which there are 33. Rare indeed are those who attain such high standing within the organization, and few members ever reach the 20th degree, much less the 33rd.

Historically, the order discouraged clerics in the society, many of whom look with disdain on the quasi-religious rituals and initiations the brotherhood performs. Some clerical leaders in the past deemed heretical the members' pledges of loyalty to other members, superceding loyalty even to a deity. In more recent years, however, the entry of priests into the Rite of Most Worthy Esoterics has increased, and as a result the vague pledges to "a higher deity" are shifting to honoring specific dwarven gods.

THE TRUE DANGER

Everything will be all right as long as the leadership and principles of the Brotherhood are not corrupted by its enemies.

KING OF BEARS

The King of Bears rules the bears and lycanthropes of the North, served by a cadre of witches and oracles. His royal court spends most of its time hunting, feasting, brawling, and drinking the finest honey mead from immense stone bowls.

QUOTE

"Ah, well. Who wants to live forever?"

USUAL LOCATION

On Gloaming Crag, in the foothills of the Reaching Mountains.

COMMON KNOWLEDGE

The rolling hills and coastal plains south of the Reaching Mountains are claimed by the Kingdom of the Bear, which has no other name in humanoid tongues. The bears (awakened, werebears, and normal bears) claim a wide region. But the population is sparse and doesn't mind trespassers, as long as they respect the King of Bears and defer to his people when challenged.

The current King of Bears is Mesikämmen, a werebear nicknamed "Old Honey Paws." He rules from Gloaming Crag, a precipice that looks like a petrified wave. Caves and tunnels riddle its interior, occupied by the king and his ursine, human, and lycanthropic retinue.

ADVENTURERS AND THE ICON

Being around the Bear King is like living in one of the Northlands' more freewheeling, high-spirited legends. Adventurers will find plenty of opportunities for daring treks, epic contests, and fierce battles against monsters of the North. Success is rewarded with rich treasure, and — even more valuable — the Bear King's loyal friendship.

ALLIES

The Bear King and First Duke-Admiral Cadua share a great mutual respect and affection — it is rumored in court that the two of them adventured together once, and they owe each other their lives. The Bear King's interest in robust trade for his realm keeps him on good terms with the Free City Council of Zobeck.

ENEMIES

Never one for reading the fine print, the Bear King once made a bargain with Baba Yaga that ended with him empty-handed and looking foolish. He angrily refuses to discuss the incident, but would love to find someone clever enough and brave enough to help him get revenge on the Feywitch.

HISTORY

Rulership of the Kingdom of the Bear is decided by yearly challenges. These opportunities are theoretically open to any bear, but lycanthropes and the awakened have an obvious advantage. Old Honey Paws has survived many of these challenges. But his reign has been so prosperous, and the Bear King himself so generally well-liked, that many of these trials by combat are undertaken simply for the honor and pleasure of fighting such a worthy opponent as the king.

Each year, many casks of mead travel north from the town of Bjeornstad in tribute to the Bear King. It is brewed by Bjeornstad's ruler, the queen Yohana Honeyhair: an elderly but still golden-haired werebear druid of the Bear Maiden. Some say that Old Honey Paws has his eye on her and may someday seek to make her his Bear Queen.

THE TRUE DANGER

Everything will be all right as long as the Bear King's desire to get back at Baba Yaga doesn't lead to a scheme that brings down the wrath of the Feywitch.

THE MASTER OF DEMON MOUNTAIN

The Master of Demon Mountain's spells and incantations carry great potency. The demons praise him, and his many children are tiefling ambassadors to the world, heralds of his power. But his real goal is to reach immortality—although first he must break the pacts binding him to Demon Mountain.

QUOTE

"So we agree? You give me your daughter and I send my pets to help you in your war, milord? Excellent!"

USUAL LOCATION

The Master is always found in Castle Dontrona on Demon Mountain.

COMMON KNOWLEDGE

The Master of Demon Mountain fled the ruins of Vael Turog hundreds of years ago and came to the Demon Mountain with little but his wits. Things changed quickly, and now his Castle Dontrona atop the sable mountain is black and gloomy, raised overnight by magic.

The Master has ruled for so long that the people of the Plains have largely forgotten his name. Out of fear or dread of drawing his attention, instead they refer to him as "the Master" or "the Sorcerer" when occasion demands they speak of him at all. The Master is a tall tiefling sorcerer with handsome features, a fine beard, bright green eyes, and black horns. His depravity simmers beneath an affected veneer of civility, and he wears a polished iron mask with accents of gold and mithral; some believe it provides the ability to see into a visitor's heart.

The Master is a creature of lascivious appetites and the father of dozens of tieflings, and his family is a source of great pride to him. They are the foundation of an empire, and his brood is loyal and as ambitious as their father. They serve him ably as his eyes, ears, and hands in distant corners of the world, since the Master seems unable or unwilling to leave his lofty castle. Instead, he sends his envoys to forge alliances through marriages or arcane trades, and then wander home along the shadow roads.

ADVENTURERS AND THE ICON

Most adventurers avoid entanglements with the Master of Demon Mountain. However, he is a being of great power and knowledge, and isn't as capricious as Baba Yaga or the Queen of Night and Magic.

ALLIES

Visitors to Demon Mountain include Baba Yaga, Exarch Vermes II, the Oracle of Kammae, and representatives of the Ghoul Emperor and the Queen of Night and Magic. One can never be sure whether any of these are true allies; but as the most powerful magical beings in Midgard, they might make bargains with the Master when it's in their interests.

ENEMIES

See "Allies" above.

HISTORY

The tall, lonely mountain south of the Wormwood forest is a spire of gray shale and red-pink granite, a barren peak standing far from the Cloudwall Mountains and topped with snow or clouds. It is a crucial landmark in the plains, and yet it seems not to belong there at all. And indeed, the Demon Mountain is a creation of magical forces and demonic will. When the Master found the conjoining ley lines at the mountain 600 years ago, he was intrigued. The place was filled with dark and demonic energies. The tsar of Vidim considered it a wasteland, a hellish blight on his southern borders. If the Master could tame it, it was his.

The sorcerer wasted no time. He summoned and bound a demonic legion and immediately staked his claim. The tsar was delighted: at last, someone had tamed the blight. The tsar gave the Master his daughter's hand in marriage in gratitude for the deed of commanding and controlling the demons. The tsar's daughter, Stasya Markova-Yodorovic, was a woman of virtue and tranquility. She bore the Master a daughter and a son, and then died in childbirth. After that, the incidents of demon raiding grew more frequent, and the tsar was no longer as fond of his former son-in-law.

Though the marriage had ended, the Master's claim to the mountain's eldritch power did not. The Master of Demon Mountain remains a figure of legend as well as a political force. But wielding worldly power and extending his influence is merely an entertaining game for him. His real goal is to reach immortality—although first he must break the pacts binding him to Demon Mountain. The pacts the Master swore to gain power over the mountain and its creatures are not the endless font of power that he had hoped. Indeed, he rarely leaves the mountain, and his children suspect he does not truly command it. Instead, the mountain commands him to bring it reagents and perform certain rituals, as demanded by demonic messengers, dreams, or priests of Chernovog.

The Master has heard from oracles that he could break his chains by marrying a bride who would bear him a son untarnished by his demonic blood—but this son must be sacrificed to the Eleven Hells. So far many of the Master's children are tainted, but the Master has found a new promising target in Irina, the beautiful daughter of the tsar of Vidim. Indeed, he has grown obsessed with Irina recently and plots to win her over.

THE TRUE DANGER

Everything will be all right as long as the Master remains bound to Demon Mountain.

THE ORACLE OF KAMMAE

The blind daughter of the moon is blessed — or cursed — with divine insight, and gifts of healing and prophecy. With the voices of spirits, angels, and canny counselors around her, the Oracle of Kammae Straboli rarely errs in matters of fact or faith.

QUOTE

"Go seven leagues to the North, to where jeweled wings beat against a blackened wall. Search among the rocks at nightfall for the hidden key — but beware the one who walks behind."

USUAL LOCATION

In the Hall of the Oracle in Kammae Straboli, adjoining the Great Gold and Silver Temple of the Three Goddesses: Hecate the Moon Goddess, Rava the Weaver of Fate, and Lada the Golden.

COMMON KNOWLEDGE

The Oracle of Kammae keeps her people safe and expects no thanks and little reward; but she treasures the few quiet hours each month when she stands with her sisters to await the new moon, before the cycle of rituals begins anew. The Oracle holds sessions for her most favored heroes and the wealthiest donors during the three days of each full moon. She traditionally sits on the ivory stairs at the center of the Great Gold and Silver Temple when receiving visions.

Entering the Hall of the Oracle is like stepping into a higher realm. The halls are heavily gilded and lit by magical lights that dim only at the new moon. Its altars are redolent of fresh flowers in summer and rich incense and lavender in winter. Tiled floors feature beautiful mosaics of fantastic creatures, enigmatic scenes laden with hermetic symbolism, and depictions of the Three Goddesses. Oracles and seers walk to and fro, lost in thought or energetically debating matters of divination and prophecy, while dream drakes look down from their high perches.

The Temple's inquisitors and paladins are members of a divine order called the Eyeless, answerable only to the Oracle, the gods, or their messengers. Their symbol is a sightless white eye, and they are both loved and feared among the people. Their elite training and zealous streak makes them dangerous to those they consider enemies of the Temple or the Oracle, though some few are corrupt. Their leader is a man named Lygren Ullos, the Dark Eye of the Moon.

ADVENTURERS AND THE ICON

As befits an icon who holds a god prisoner, the Oracle of Kammae's quests often attract the attention of divine powers — or challenge them directly. Adventurers might battle monsters from the dawn of time, trade riddles with an immortal shrine guardian, or call forth a forgotten deity in a ruined temple. But the Oracle is also a head of state, with very real earthly concerns. She may need adventurers for missions against a rival city-state, or she may need outsiders to investigate corruption among her priests and oracles.

ALLIES

The Oracle of Kammae gained much when she chained Nethus, but she also lost many of her allies. Among these allies, the Oracle has a strong mystical connection to Baba Yaga through the mysteries of the Moon Goddess.

ENEMIES

The Dragon Sultana's Mharoti empire represents a grave threat to Kammae and the rest of the Seven Cities. The Queen of Night and Magic is the Oracle's rival for the adoration of those who revere shadow and the arcane; and she maintains a long-standing feud with First Duke-Admiral Cadua of Triolo over the chaining of Nethus.

HISTORY

Like many of her sisters in the Great Gold and Silver Temple, Yeneva Podella was an orphan raised in the faith—but her gifts shone through from an early age. She would often startle visitors with detailed knowledge of events in distant realms, or deeds done in secret. Her predictions of the future were unerring, though sometimes they took time and effort to interpret. Word of the young girl's talents spread, and her influence quickly grew as she became indispensable to the wealthy and powerful of Kammae Straboli.

Yeneva's divinely-granted knowledge of things to come gave her the serenity–and ruthlessness–of absolute confidence in the rightness of her actions. Before she was 40 years old Yeneva had gone from advising the city's rulers to ruling Kammae as its Oracle.

Fifteen years ago the Oracle's soldiers attacked and kidnapped the sea god Nethus, magically chaining him as a prisoner. Today the Temple of Nethus in Kammae is guarded at all times by minotaurs with axes and inquisitors with questions for those who pass by too closely. The interior is not open to worshipers, and the god's name is rarely spoken. Oracles, priests of the Moon Goddess, and privileged visitors can speak to the god through magical means, receiving divine blessings, power, and information.

Despite such protections, some have found their own ways into the temple. The huginn seer-poet and adventurer Drouin "Croak-eye" Stroud, known as the Songraven, is nicknamed the "Rascal of Kammae" because he talked his way past the jailers of Nethus to trade secrets with the chained god.

The battle that enslaved and chained Nethus inflicted other casualties, most of all the sea god's wife Mnemosyne. The Kammaen inquisitors removed from her mind any trace of their crime and the methods they used to capture Nethus. They also cursed the handmaidens and servants who sought to protect her into horrid forms. Now they travel throughout Midgard in disguise, seeking the details of Nethus's capture in hopes of restoring the memories of their queen.

THE TRUE DANGER

Everything will be all right (for the Oracle, at least) as long as Mnemosyne never succeeds in freeing Nethus. If she does, the wrath of the sea god toward the Oracle and her people will be mighty indeed.

QUEEN OF NIGHT AND MAGIC

The Queen of Night and Magic rules the Shadow Realm, where she dreams of conquest, blood, and loss. She remembers too many worlds that once were hers.

QUOTE

"We will tolerate many things, child of the day. Poor manners are not among them."

USUAL LOCATION

Within her palace of glass and dreams in the Shadow Realm, attended by 1,000 fey lords and ladies with alabaster skin and hearts of ice.

COMMON KNOWLEDGE

Her Celestial and Royal Majesty Sarastra Aestruum, Queen of Night and Magic, rules the Shadow Realm, the source of darkness and arcane energies. Her Moonlit King is rarely seen but is feared even among the shadow fey.

The Queen weaves her plots out of boredom and malice; her mastery of the arcane and her control of deceptions and misdirection make her highly dangerous. She has a perfect memory for the slightest insult, and some of her revenges take centuries to complete.

ADVENTURERS AND THE ICON

The Queen's attention is dangerous, but can bring great reward to those who please her—a difficult prospect given her mercurial moods. Some of her missions resemble quests out of an old fairy tale: retrieve a magic wand from a bottomless pool, find a transformed prince or awaken a sleeping fey beauty. Others are capricious and cruel. For example, a party may be tasked with ruining the life of someone whose ancestor failed to address her by her full title 300 years ago.

If the Queen finds an adventurer attractive she may take him or her as a lover, until she grows bored and discards her quickly-forgotten toy.

Unless they magically travel to the Winter Court, adventurers will deal with royal ambassadors such as Thelamandrine, the Hidden Ambassador to Zobeck. They might meet the queen's relatives, such as the Black Prince of the Scàthsidhe in the Empire of the Ghouls. Lord Fandorin of Morgau and Doresh is believed to follow the Goddess of Night and Magic.

ALLIES

Sarastra counts Baba Yaga as a friend and ally, and subtly influences the Ghoul Emperor through her representative the Black Prince.

ENEMIES

The Free Council of Zobeck permits trade with the Shadow Realm, but will never forget that Sarastra granted House Stross its mastery of shadow magic. (After the events in **Courts of the Shadow Fey**, the Free Council is *extremely* unhappy about the Queen's designs on their city.) Linked through Hecate, the Oracle of Kammae and the Queen are rivals for the love and adoration of those who revere night and magic.

HISTORY

No one knows for certain when Sarastra, the daughter of High Queen Lelliana Thorntree Endiamon of the elves, was exiled to Shadow or why. But since that long-ago day, she has ruled from her dark throne of gold-flecked lapis lazuli as the Queen and Goddess of Night and Magic, attended by goblins, sprites, talking animals, demons, and her cold and malevolent children, the shadow fey.

1,400 years ago, the Holly King and his fey followers sacrificed a young woman on Rosehaven Hill in the Margreve forest, and planted a black oak on the site. This ritual, meant to steal Sarastra's power, was a trap set by the Shadow Princess herself. A powerful curse transported them all into the Plane of Shadow, where Sarastra forced them into servitude. The Heartwood Pact also connected the black oak, the hill, and the castle Shadowcrag that would later stand upon it, with the Shadow Plane.

To protect the oak, the Queen allied herself with the ambitious human Stross family. In exchange for fostering their eldest daughters and eldest sons in the courts of the shadow fey, the Stross learned shadow magic and gained the right to rule the Rosehaven lands—as the fey called the small walled city of Zobeck and the kobold mines around it.

Sarastra next enters history during the Black Sorceress' Revolt against the elves, nearly 800 years ago. When the fey roads became corrupted, the Queen and her shadow fey foresaw the end of elven rule in Midgard and allied themselves with the dark powers summoned by the mages of Caelmarath.

When House Stross fell in Zobeck's Great Revolt, the Queen and her people faded from mortal memory for nearly 80 years. Then two merchants of Zobeck, inspired by bards' tales of the fey and aided by an Arcane Collegium linguist, succeeded in establishing trade with the Shadow Realm. Since that time the Chartered Merchants of Scáthesidhe have conveyed moonlight steel and mirrors to Zobeck direct from the fey lands. Other caravans now brave the shadow road each year, returning with riches and wonders never before seen.

For these isolated and dangerous fey, trade with the mortal world presents the greatest opportunity in many bleak years. The Shadow Realm is stirring, and the Queen of Night and Magic's power grows.

THE TRUE DANGER

Everything will be all right as long as the Queen cannot seal the bargain she wants most: one that will give her dominion over her old lands in the Margreve, and perhaps eventually, all of Midgard.

OPEN GAME LICENSE Version 1.0a

CPSIA information can be obtained at www.ICGtesting.com
Printed in the USA
LVOW03s1442200614

391003LV00012B/325/P